The Young Evangelicals

THE YOUNG EVANGELICALS

Revolution in Orthodoxy

RICHARD QUEBEDEAUX

HARPER & ROW, PUBLISHERS
New York, Evanston, San Francisco, London

Acknowledgments

Acknowledgment is gratefully made to the following for permission to include copyrighted materials:

Campus Crusade for Christ, Inc. for quotations from *The Four Spiritual Laws*. Copyright © 1965 by Campus Crusade for Christ, Inc.

Creation House, Inc. for quotations from *The Cross & The Flag*, Robert G. Clouse, Robert D. Linder, and Richard V. Pierard, eds. Copyright © 1962 by Creation House, Inc.

InterVarsity Press for quotations from *Christ the Liberator* by John R. W. Stott, *et al.* Copyright © 1971 by Inter-Varsity Christian Fellowship.

Macmillan Publishing Co., Inc., and SCM Press, Ltd., London, for quotations from *The Cost of Discipleship* by Dietrich Bonhoeffer (2nd edition). Copyright © 1959 by SCM Press, Ltd.

Macmillan Publishing Co., Inc., and Collins Publishers, London, for quotations from *Mere Christianity* by C. S. Lewis. Copyright 1943, 1945, 1952 by Macmillan Publishing Co., Inc.

Grateful acknowledgment is also made to the editor of *The Other Side* for permission to reprint "23 Psalm of the Black Man" by Donald Oden, and to the editors of *The Post-American* for permission to quote from various issues of that publication.

Unless otherwise noted, the Scripture quotations in this publication are from the Revised Standard Version Bible, copyrighted 1946 (renewed 1973), 1952 and © 1971 by the Division of Christian Education of the National Council of the Churches of Christ in the U.S.A., and used by permission.

Portions of this book originally appeared in the December 27, 1971 issue of *Christianity and Crisis*. Copyright © 1971 by Christianity and Crisis.

Library of Congress Cataloging in Publication Data

Quebedeaux, Richard
    The young evangelicals.

    Bibliography: p.
    1. Evangelicalism. I. Title.
BR1640.Q42   269'.2   73–6344
ISBN 0–06–066725–7

To John Coleman Bennett

For some very helpful advice that led,
ultimately, to this book

Christianity is emphatically a social religion. Its teaching is directed to men not as units isolated from their fellows but as members of groups and communities. . . . It asserts that the relations of men to one another are part of their relation to God. . . . These relations are, of course, of many different kinds. But in the case of the majority of men they are determined more directly and continuously by the action of economic interests than by any other single force. It is clearly the duty of Christians, therefore, to test by the canons of their faith not merely their individual conduct and the quality of their private lives, but also the institutional framework of organized society.

*The Oxford Conference:
Official Report* (1937)

Contents

Preface

Theology is a bag of tricks. Just a few years after God's most recent funeral, he has again shown himself to be alive and well. But then resurrection *is* an important—though often unexpected—part of divine activity. This book is about a thoroughly resurrected Christian Orthodoxy—so different from its stereotype, so dynamic, that it can only be termed revolutionary.

As one who considers himself a participant in the present revolution in Orthodoxy—as a Young Evangelical—I have written this account for the informed layperson, and not without an Evangelical purpose in mind. Part of what I say is based upon the sum total of my own experiences (and those of numerous friends and acquaintances from similar backgrounds) rather than documentary evidence. In fact, the book is, indirectly, a spiritual autobiography. Furthermore, I am not particularly concerned that the reader agree with my convictions, but rather that he or she will be motivated to think seriously about the points I raise, then act accordingly. And although the specific problems addressed here tend to be basically American in nature, I am convinced that these same issues (in one form or another) are also alive in other countries where Fundamentalism, Liberalism, and Evangelicalism—no less than Protestantism and Catholicism—have divided the Church and to this day do not peacefully coexist.

Over the course of years, many individuals—by way of teaching, conversations and correspondence—have stimulated my thinking concerning the emerging generation of Young Evangelicals and related topics (and have otherwise helped me set forth my ideas in writing). These persons include Dr. Leslie Agnew of UCLA; Lois Bright of Logos

Isla Vista, Goleta, California; the Rev. Lee Carlton of MCC Los Angeles; David Gill, formerly of CWLF; the Rev. Peter Gomes of the Harvard Memorial Church; Dr. Harold Kuhn of Asbury Theological Seminary; the Rev. Grant Lee of Honolulu; Dennis MacDonald of the People's Christian Coalition; John Nordquist of Santa Monica, California; Dr. Paul Ramsey of Princeton University; Dr. Herbert Richardson of St. Michael's College, Toronto; Dr. Krister Stendahl of the Harvard Divinity School; John Strandness of Portland, Oregon; the Rev. Rodney Toews of Gospel Light Publications, Glendale, California; Andrew Walls of the University of Aberdeen, Scotland; Carolyn Johnson Winston of Honolulu; and the Rev. Dick Young, formerly of IVCF staff.

To the following individuals, I would like to offer special thanks for their advice and encouragement: the Reverend Simeon Adebola of Lagos, Nigeria; the Rev. Chuck Doak, UMHE Campus Pastor at UCLA; the Rev. George Exoo of Washington and Jefferson College, Washington, Pennsylvania; the Rev. Gene Langevin of Quincy, Massachusetts; Randy Neal of Logos Westwood, Los Angeles; Henry Pearson of Nottingham, England; Dr. Bryan Wilson of All Souls College, Oxford, my doctoral thesis supervisor; and my parents, Thomas and Annette Quebedeaux, who provided generous financial assistance for this project. But I reserve for myself the responsibility for all my mistakes.

Richard Quebedeaux

Long Beach, California

The Young Evangelicals

I. Introduction: The Contemporary Evangelical Movement

Except a man be born again, he cannot see the kingdom of God.

John 3:3 (KJV)

For if a man is in Christ he becomes a new person altogether—the past is finished and gone, everything has become fresh and new. All this is God's doing, for he has reconciled us to himself through Jesus Christ; and he has made us agents of the reconciliation.

II Corinthians 5:17, 18
(J. B. Phillips)

To describe an evangelical is to describe a state of mind, a religious posture, a way of looking at spiritual reality. There is no doctrinal unity among them and one trait which might characterize many would be vehemently rejected by others.

Kilian McDonnell, O.S.B.,
Commonweal

Secularization has recently become a very important word in the theological vocabulary. Harvey Cox in *The Secular City* (N.Y: Macmillan Paperbacks, 1965) defines secularization simply as "the liberation of man from religious . . . tutelage, the turning of his attention away from other worlds toward this one" (page 17). By the mid-1960s, even theologians had come to accept—if not celebrate—the secular understanding of the Gospel, of man and his world. Today there is no point in challenging the assumption that ours is a secular culture, that a religious world view is no longer dominant as the frame of reference for thought. Nevertheless, we *are* justified in arguing that something is happening on the contemporary scene which indicates that modern man might not, in fact, be so utterly free of religious needs and aspirations as was hitherto supposed. The current rediscovery of the supernatural, the upsurge in popularity of Eastern religious traditions and the occult, the renaissance of Evangelical and enthusiastic Christianity—affecting all strata of Western society—together point to the re-emergence of what Andrew Greeley calls *"unsecular man."*

If the design religion gives to life is looked upon by the skeptic as a set of rules and practices conceived to make sense out of chance events and cosmic indifference to human concerns, that same design is viewed by the believer as a revelation of the deeper meaning of experience— something which is at the very heart of religion. The religious experience is nothing less than an attempt by men and women to respond to and enter into a relationship with what lies behind and beyond mere appearance—with God himself.

Yet, basic to the essence of religion is an unavoidable dilemma. Religious persons must always live in relationship with two contrary realms of experience. They must relate both to the sacred and to the profane. And they must concern themselves both with the ultimate and the mundane, the spirit and the flesh. Out of this situation comes a multitude of problems for the Church of all ages, not the least of which is the persistent effort to preserve the spirit of the New Testament and the primitive church in the changing conditions of each ensuing generation.[1] It is in this context that we shall examine closely one particularly energetic attempt to maintain and renew that spirit—the contemporary *Evangelical movement.*

A. EVANGELICALISM

In its widest sense, *Evangelicalism* is nothing new. Granting the variety of meanings appropriate to the word in different historical and cultural contexts, Evangelicalism has most often been associated with the doctrine of salvation by faith in Christ alone. During the Reformation, the followers of Martin Luther, stressing this singular faith, were generally called Evangelicals to distinguish them from the Calvinists, who were designated as *Reformed*. Indeed, a good number of Lutheran synods both in Europe and the United States still use the term Evangelical in their official nomenclature.

The Evangelical revival in the eighteenth century was represented by pietism in Germany, Methodism in England, and the Great Awakening in America. Since that time, especially in English-speaking countries, Evangelicalism has been looked upon as the school of Protestant Christianity affirming salvation through faith in the atoning death of Christ and denying any saving efficacy either in good works or in the sacraments. This Evangelical tradition, which has included both a wing of the Anglican communion and churches that developed as a result of the eighteenth-century Evangelical revival, also regarded as central tenets of the Christian faith the inspiration and authority of the Bible, man's inherent depravity, and the more or less symbolic nature of the sacraments. In its worship, moreover, heavy importance has been placed upon evangelistic preaching and the reading of Scripture.

The Evangelical party in England had more in common with Nonconformists than with the High Church wing of its own communion. This fact led to frequent expressions of cooperation between the Anglican Evangelicals and the Nonconformists both in social welfare and in the missionary endeavors of the nineteenth century. During the same period, similar alliances took place in the United States among the Protestant churches.

With the division between *Modernists* or *Liberals* (interchangeable terms, though the former is now less frequently used) and *Fundamentalists* in the early twentieth century, particularly in America, Evangelicalism took on another shade of meaning. After 1940, *Neo-Evangelicalism* became recognizable in the United States as a strong force within conservative Christianity—one which holds firm to what it believes is biblical or historic Orthodoxy but at the same time repudiates the theological and cultural excesses of Fundamentalism.

This contemporary Evangelicalism is by no means unified in the fine points (and even some of the not-so-fine points) of doctrine. But it can now be characterized as a school of Christianity which attests to the truth of three major theological principles: (1) the complete reliability and final authority of Scripture in matters of faith and practice; (2) the necessity of a *personal* faith in Jesus Christ as Savior from sin and consequent commitment to Him as Lord; and (3) the urgency of seeking actively the conversion of sinners to Christ. Among different Evangelical scholars and groups, to be sure, these three points are variously interpreted, but their basic truth is always upheld.

For the Evangelical, Christian faith is *experiential*. Knowing Christ, like knowing any person on a deep level, is an experience; and the new birth which He provides marks the beginning of a growing experience. Nevertheless, the Christian experience does not take place in a vacuum; for it is in the words of the Bible that a man or woman comes, ultimately, face to face with the claims of Christ on his or her life.

Evangelicalism transcends denominations and their respective polities. Furthermore, it can well be termed an ideologically conservative *movement* rather than a church or denomination. Evangelicalism is conservative insofar as it differs from Liberalism, which either denies or bypasses the three basic theological principles Evangelicalism affirms. It is a movement in the sense that Evangelicalism embraces numbers of people who are united—spiritually at least—in a concerted effort on a common project with some degree of organization. Although Evangelicals are, in fact, organized in many different ways, and their unity is clearly imperfect, the common goal of evangelizing the world for Christ, of seeking the conversion of sinners, does bind them together in that task.

Finally, Evangelicalism is rooted firmly in what it understands as *historic* or *biblical Orthodoxy*. The late Edward John Carnell of Fuller Theological Seminary, one of the most highly respected Evangelical apologists, describes Orthodoxy in *The Case for Biblical Christianity* (Ronald H. Nash, ed. Grand Rapids: Eerdmans, 1969) as "that branch of Christendom which limits the ground of religious authority to the Bible" (p. 168). According to Carnell, Orthodoxy does not invariably have all the answers; nor does it always ask the right questions. And its claims are often corrupted by bad manners. Nevertheless, beneath these outer garments is the conviction that the testimony of Christ is the ultimate norm for the Church. And included in that testimony is the assurance that the written Word is inspired by God and, therefore, has the force of law. For the Evangelical, any theological stance which does not accept the inspiration and authority of Scripture cannot rightly call itself Orthodox.

B. THE GREAT PROTESTANT SCHISM

To understand contemporary Evangelicalism, we must first know something about its historical roots and the developments within modern Christianity that led to its emergence. Specifically, we shall have to turn our attention to the *Fundamentalist–Modernist controversy* of the 1920s and 30s, its background and consequences. For it was that dispute which divided Protestantism in America into two hostile camps and resulted in a factionalism within the Church from which it has never fully recovered.

During the course of years immediately following the Civil War and thereafter, dramatic changes in the intellectual climate of the United States became manifestly apparent. The issues raised influenced the shape of Protestant theology profoundly, since they constituted a serious threat to accepted understandings of the Christian faith. The fresh psychological and sociological studies of scholars like William James and William Graham Sumner tended to reduce religion to a mere social phenomenon. As an emerging academic discipline, the comparative study of religion raised questions about the uniqueness of Christian faith. Darwinian biology and the new biblical studies, including *higher criticism* stemming mainly from German universities, seemed to undermine the authority of the Bible.

According to Winthrop S. Hudson, in *Religion in America* (N.Y.: Scribners, 1965), the response among Protestants to the challenge of scientific modes of thought moved in three different directions—not without lasting results. Some rejected the new intellectual currents more or less completely and refused to modify their inherited theological formulations at all. Others came to believe that the traditional expressions of faith were entirely outmoded and had to be replaced by views and practices seemingly demanded by a scientific world view. This was the radical response. A third stream tried hard to accommodate itself to the novel patterns of thought by adjusting elements of the inherited religious tradition accordingly. The radically iconoclastic tendency was never very popular on the American scene. But significant and often quite uncritical theological accommodation to the new intellectual trends was destined to flourish as Liberalism, while, already during the late nineteenth century, the forces of reaction became increasingly dominant in Protestant Orthodoxy.

Roughly parallel to the development of a fresh intellectual climate in America with its strong influence on theology was the emergence of Social Christianity or, as it was later called, the *Social Gospel*. Stimulated by English, German, and Swiss Christian Socialism and the increasingly visible problems associated with technological advance, urbanization, and expanded immigration, many Liberal (and some Orthodox) ministers and theologians began *emphasizing* the social application of the Gospel. The new biblical criticism, if it deprecated the supernatural elements in Scripture and the "predictive" sense of prophecy, at the same time stressed the *ethical* teachings of the Old Testament prophets and Jesus himself. Supported by the general optimism of the age, Liberal pastors and seminary professors espoused the centrality of the kingdom of God in Christian doctrine. Inherent in their interpretation of the kingdom was a belief, later considered naïve, that the kingdom of God could, in fact, be established on earth primarily, if not exclusively, by the efforts of men and women working for political and social reform. For these clergymen and religious thinkers, social salvation was often *the* message of the Gospel.

By the beginning of World War I, the Social Gospel had growing popular and official support. Social concern had reshaped the curricula of seminaries, some of which moved from peaceful, isolated communities to troubled urban areas in the process. Almost all the major denominations had established departments or commissions for social action. In 1908, the Federal Council of Churches (predecessor of the National Council of Churches) was formed largely to enable the churches, by joint endeavors, to deal more effectively with the problems of an industrial society. Indeed, one of the first acts of the new council was its adoption of a "Social Creed of the Churches." Social Gospel ideology ranged from the mild progressivism of Washington Gladden to the demand for a radical reconstruction of society voiced by George Herron. But at its deepest level the Social Gospel was basically a manifestation of middle-class idealism. For the Liberals, the social dimension of the Gospel, with its almost exclusive attention to the horizontal needs of man in society and its neglect of the vertical desires of the heart for God, became orthodox Christianity.

The increasing accommodation within Protestantism to the new intellectual climate was resisted vigorously by conservatives on the basis of their view of biblical inerrancy, since the central issue was clearly the authority of Scripture. Unfortunately, the Orthodox response was chiefly limited to uncreative denials based upon a theological indifference to the fresh scientific studies. Liberalism had begun to permeate almost all denominations except the Lutherans and Southern Baptists. But even they were not left untouched. Because of their loose form of government, the Congregationalists and Northern (now American) Baptists usually offered a haven for the growing liberal sentiment. Especially among northern Presbyterians, vocally liberal ministers and seminary professors became defendants in the notorious heresy trials of the late nineteenth century. Those convicted often lost both their ecclesiastical standing and their jobs. Yet the trials failed to halt the further penetration of Liberalism within denominational ranks and served rather to awaken popular sympathy for the persecuted.

By the time of the outbreak of World War I, the theological climate of the nation varied considerably from section to section. New England and New York were bastions of Liberalism. The Midwest, though it harbored both radicals of the left and right, was generally moderate. The South and Pacific Coast could be described as basically conservative.

During the period from the late nineteenth century to the beginning of World War I, two rival schools of Orthodoxy emerged on the American scene. The first, originally centered mainly in New Jersey and Pennsylvania, was a Presbyterianism fashioned by the unyielding Orthodoxy of Western, Pittsburgh, and Princeton Theological Seminaries. Archibald Alexander Hodge (1823–86) and Benjamin Warfield (1851–1921), both firm adherents to the Westminster Confession of Faith (1646), shaped the "Princeton Doctrine of Inspiration" which soon became a major apologetic for biblical inerrancy. Princeton Orthodoxy was both vigorous and articulate and did not easily fall prey to the kind of anti-intellectualism often characteristic of its similarly Orthodox rival.

Meanwhile, beginning in the northern half of the United States, there developed a second school of Orthodoxy which would greatly strengthen the forces of conservative Christianity. Known as *Dispensationalism*, this Orthodox school of theology was based upon the speculations of J. N. Darby (1800–82) in England. It was carried throughout America by itinerant evangelists, popularized at prophetic Bible conferences held annually after 1876, and given leadership by faculty and graduates of the newly established Bible schools (survivals of which include the Moody Bible Institute in Chicago and the Bible Institute of Los Angeles, now called Biola College). Dispensationalism made inroads in practically all Protestant denominations, and its popularity was facilitated by the appearance of the *Scofield Reference Bible* (1909), an annotated edition of the Scriptures prepared largely by C. I. Scofield which imposed a rigid schematization and periodization on the biblical materials by relating every part of the Bible to a timetable of *dispensations*, each of which signifies a different way in which God relates to man. Inherent in this theological stance was a feeling that all established denominations had become apostate, and true Christians, therefore, would do well to separate themselves from those inclusive ecclesiastical bodies. Partly as a reaction to Liberalism's denial of the predictive sense of prophecy in favor of the ethical, Dispensationalism literalized to an extreme the prophetic portions of Scripture and accepted no other form of interpretation. Furthermore, the Dispensationalists branded as a work of Satan *any* manifestation of what seemed to them theological liberalism. Most Protestant conservatives hesitated to identify themselves with the Bible-school men as a result; nevertheless, they did, on occasion, welcome their support when very important issues were at stake.

But what about the Orthodox response to the Social Gospel? Most (but not all) conservative preachers and academics were too busy holding revivals and Bible conferences and defending the faith to be concerned with the social application of the Gospel. Moreover, their hard-line defensiveness and general disapproval of the Liberals who *were* active in confronting the human problems of industrialization led, obviously, to a mounting criticism of the Social Gospel as a whole. So, the stage was set for the showdown which was to be known as the Fundamentalist–Modernist controversy.

In 1910, there appeared in print ten small volumes entitled *The Fundamentals: A Testimony to the Truth*. This work, edited by Amzi

Dixon (1854–1925) and Reuben Archer Torrey (1856–1928) of the Moody Bible Institute and Church, attempted to reduce the Christian faith to a number of easily understandable essentials. The small treatises set forth several doctrines, five of which came to be known popularly as "fundamentals of the faith," namely: (1) the verbal inspiration of the Bible, (2) the virgin birth of Christ, (3) his substitutionary atonement, (4) his bodily resurrection, and (5) his imminent and visible Second Coming. These volumes were sent free to ministers, evangelists, missionaries, Sunday school superintendents, theological students and the like, until three million copies had been distributed. The cost involved was borne by two wealthy Los Angeles businessmen, Milton and Lyman Stewart. Unquestionably the work was significant, since it led ultimately to the establishment of a doctrinal basis by some of the most powerful voices of Orthodoxy not only in America, but in Canada, England, Ireland and Germany as well.

Before the 1920s, the Fundamentalists tended to be loosely organized in a multitude of rather undisciplined groups. But early in that decade, somewhat successful attempts at better organization were undertaken. Nineteen twenty-five was indeed a climactic year for the Fundamentalists with the Scopes monkey trial held at Dayton, Tennessee. John Scopes, a mild-mannered schoolteacher, had been arrested for violating a Tennessee statute forbidding the teaching of evolution in tax-supported schools of the state. Although Scopes was, in fact, found guilty, this comical episode with its smear tactics, violent language and obscurantism, attracted national and world attention, and in no way helped the Fundamentalist cause. Noted for their general divisiveness and discordance, the Fundamentalists, when not fighting the Modernists or Liberals, took sides against Roman Catholics, secular evolutionists, and most important, they fought unceasingly among themselves. The fact that these conservatives seemed utterly incapable of cooperative action constitutes one major reason why the Fundamentalists lost every ecclesiastical battle they undertook.

In 1929, the scholarly J. Gresham Machen (1881–1937) of Princeton Theological Seminary resigned from its faculty to form a more Orthodox school of theology, Westminster Theological Seminary. Later, in 1933, Machen also led the formation of an independent missions board which would recruit only conservative missionary candidates. This action was regarded by the Presbyterian Church as a clear case of insubordination, and Machen was expelled from the denomination in 1936. Having just laid the groundwork for a new ecclesiastical structure, he died early in 1937. And within only six months of his death, the newly emerging denomination divided in two. One group founded the Orthodox Presbyterian Church, in line with Machen's general philosophy; another party, led by Carl McIntire, organized the more separatist Bible Presbyterian Church and its official school of theology, Faith Theological Seminary.

Most other denominations continued to be troubled by controversy throughout the 1930s and later as well. A case in point is the schisms that depleted the ranks of the American (Northern) Baptists during that period. In 1932, a dissident group withdrew to form the General Association of Regular Baptists (GARB); and fifteen years later, the organization of the less separatist Conservative Baptist Association (CBA) took place.

While Fundamentalism was declining during these years as a strong force to reckon with in the major denominations, it *was* able to keep itself very much alive in many local congregations. Furthermore, the movement even extended its influence by the formation of independent Bible churches and the capture of various smaller ecclesiastical bodies. To fill the vacant Fundamentalist pulpits, graduates of the numerous Bible institutes and colleges which had arisen throughout the nation were recruited as pastors. By World War II, side by side with the mainstream denominations and their instrumentalities, there existed *separate* Fundamentalist colleges and seminaries, publishers and periodicals, missionary and evangelistic associations, boards and councils of churches. But Fundamentalism was still most often linked with the anti-intellectualism, bad manners, and obscurantism that had been so much a part of its heritage.

During the period of time in which the Fundamentalist–Modernist controversy raged on, and Fundamentalism failed in its attempt to capture (or recapture) the historic Protestant denominations, Liberalism itself had undergone significant ideological changes. The manifest horrors of the First World War, and later the Second, provided the impetus for a theological reconstruction in the wake of a declining Social Gospel which did not understand the radical nature of sin and was therefore unable to speak with force to a nation and world whose optimism had been shattered by the realities of global military conflict.

It was in the 1930s, in the seminaries, that the theological revival in America began in earnest. Motivated largely by the thinking of scholars like Karl Barth and Emil Brunner in Europe, and Reinhold Niebuhr in the United States, the new, more conservative theology was generally labeled *Neo-Orthodoxy*. Several characteristic themes in that theological stance gradually became apparent.

First, counter to the old Liberal notion of immanence which stressed the presence of God in us and the identification of God with the goodness of the world and equated divine activity with the accomplishment of human goals, there was a reassertion of God's transcendence or otherness and his sovereignty over creation. Man could no longer be master of his own destiny, a role the Social Gospel had seemed quite willing to give him.

Second, the naïvely optimistic evaluation of the human situation prevalent in the late nineteenth and early twentieth centuries was systematically demolished by two world wars and the inhumanity of men like Hitler and Stalin. Once again the power of sin had to be taken seriously. The confident expectation that the social order could be progressively transformed into the kingdom of God by the efforts of men and women alone was repudiated. It came to be realized that no one social or political system is free from human finitude, or not subject to change into an instrument of power for the sake of whichever group should become dominant. God's judgment was discerned to fall upon *all* social structures and programs, and no one program of reform (political or otherwise) could simply be identified with the will of God.

Third, there came about a new interest in biblical revelation. Further historical studies and the findings of archeology led to a new appreciation of the Bible, not as revelation *itself*, but as the record of men of faith who had witnessed the "mighty acts of God in history," the most definitive of which was the "event" of Jesus Christ. It was not the words of Scripture, but God's deeds in history, discerned by the community of faith, that were accepted as revelatory. The Bible is merely the testimony to that divine revelation. This fresh understanding of Scripture emerged when it was clear that the earlier biblical criticism had been as much the product of a now outmoded nineteenth-century German idealism as anything else and that the historical elements in the Bible had wrongfully been neglected.

Fourth, a renewed attention to Christology was evident. If the words of Scripture constituted a faithful witness to Jesus Christ, the *living* Word, then he could be encountered personally in the Bible through the power of the Holy Spirit working on the reader or hearer.

Finally, there was a tendency to seek the recovery of a lost wholeness or fullness in the life of a divided Church. It had long been apparent that the extensive foreign missionary endeavors of the nineteenth and twentieth centuries were weakened spiritually by denominational competition and rivalry among missionaries on the field. This very practical issue was one major factor in the growing desire to somehow restore basic Christian unity both on the home front and overseas—a wish which resulted ultimately in the Ecumenical movement. *(Ecumenical* comes from the Greek *oikoumenē* [i.e., inhabited earth]. Upon the analogy of the application of the term *oikoumenē* to the Greek [and later to the Roman] world, the Ecumenical movement designates the contemporary attempt to restore Christian unity throughout the inhabited globe.) In 1908, the Federal Council of Churches (which became the National Council of Churches in 1950) was established. Later, in 1948, the World Council of Churches was organized in Geneva. Added to these conciliar Ecumenical efforts were various denominational mergers and the new rapprochement with the Roman Catholic Church effected by Vatican II.

While Neo-Orthodoxy was making its impact on American Liberalism, a more conciliatory school of thought was taking shape within Fundamentalism. Led by a handful of younger theologians, this dynamic expression of Orthodox Christianity became known as *Evangelicalism* to distinguish itself from the extreme separatism, bad manners, obscurantism and anti-intellectualism so characteristic of Fundamentalism, but not from the Fundamentalist insistence on the authority and inspiration of Scripture, the necessity of conversion, and the mandate for evangelism.

In 1942, under the leadership of Harold John Ockenga (now president of Gordon-Conwell Theological Seminary), the National Association of Evangelicals (NAE) was formed to bring together the forces of Neo-Evangelicalism in a common cause—to penetrate the historic denominations by persuasion from within rather than by criticism from without.

During the course of the 1940s and 50s, there emerged a number of highly educated Evangelical thinkers such as Edward John Carnell and Carl F. H. Henry, who were determined to develop a rational and philosophic apologetic for historic and biblical Orthodoxy, and who were at the same time willing to engage in constructive theological debate with the exponents of contrary views. The scholarly interests of Evangelicalism resulted in the founding of *Christianity Today* in 1956. Carl Henry became the first editor of this conservative counterpart to *The Christian Century* and *Christianity and Crisis* which was to become the official periodical voice of the new Evangelicals.

Also closely associated with the rise of Evangelicalism has been the career of Billy Graham. Graham had originally been recruited in 1945 by Youth for Christ (an organization of Evangelical young people established in 1943) to serve as an itinerant evangelist for its Saturday night rallies. After his successful revival campaigns in Los Angeles in 1949, and Portland, Oregon, in 1950, Graham was clearly on his way to national and world notoriety. Early in his ministry, Graham modified his initial sensationalism and condemned denominational feuds and the intolerance and separatism of the Fundamentalists. Soon the handsome and personally attractive evangelist was to rise to prominence as the foremost recruiter for Evangelical Christianity and its most popular spokesman.

Evangelicalism, as we have mentioned, repudiated the distasteful cultural and social elements of Fundamentalism. Its criticism of the old Liberalism was similar to the critique leveled by Neo-Orthodoxy, but it found the Neo-Orthodox stance inadequate as well on at least three major points.

First, Neo-Orthodoxy did not accept the inspiration and authority of the Bible or recognize its words as revelation itself. For that school of theology, Scripture was understood merely as the *witness* to Jesus Christ who alone was regarded as the authority for the Church. But Evangelicals found the authority of Christ, as a doctrine, far too nebulous and thus too difficult to apply to the concrete issues of the Christian faith. And if the authority of Jesus Christ is to be discerned within the community of faith, as Neo-Orthodoxy suggested, *which* community's understanding is to become normative? Carl McIntire's? Norman Vincent Peale's? Oral Roberts's? In this connection, the whole notion of God's revelatory acts in history seemed to pose a difficult problem for the Evangelicals. Exactly *how* are the mighty acts of God to be identified within the complexities of history? Where, in any given historical act, is the *locus* of revelation to be found? And finally, in what way does that locus relate to God?

A second weakness of Neo-Orthodoxy apparent to the Evangelicals was its sidestepping of the conversion question. Implicit here was the doctrine of universal salvation most readily perceived in Karl Barth. In Neo-Orthodox theology, the Church does have an obligation to proclaim the lordship of Christ; but this proclamation rests on the underlying assumption that the world is, in fact, already reconciled to God. People who are not yet aware of God's mighty deed of reconciling the whole human race would benefit from this knowledge of what God had accomplished. Yet, in Neo-Orthodoxy, there seemed to be no real *requirement* that a man repent and believe the Gospel. Even the existential encounter with Christ emphasized in Neo-Orthodox circles tended to function simply as a vague and vacuous religious experience.

Its bypassing of the necessity of conversion led to a third inadequacy in Neo-Orthodoxy discerned by the Evangelicals. If the world has already been reconciled to God, as Neo-Orthodox theology implied, why bother about personal evangelism at all? This question was answered by a reinterpretation of the whole concept of evangelism. In place of the traditional proclamation that all men and women are sinners who need a new birth through personal commitment to Christ as Savior, the new evangelism would be a prophetic call for the creation of a just and equitable society throughout the world compatible with the universal new humanity called into being by God. Evangelicals insisted, however, that only men and women who had been born again and thus were personally transformed by the Spirit of God were adequately equipped to build a more righteous national and world order—a proposition which has only recently been challenged within the ranks of Evangelicalism itself.

Lacking a firm basis of authority from which to operate, and neglecting traditional evangelism, Neo-Orthodoxy passed out of existence as a viable school of Christian thought with the advent in the mid-1960s of a new radical Liberalism or secular Christianity which now seems to be the dominant ideological stance of what we shall term *mainstream Ecumenical Liberalism*. In the seminaries and the Ecumenical structures, there emerged a generation of younger theologians who had become impatient with Neo-Orthodoxy's pessimism concerning the human situation and its slowness to implement a program for social and political change. The pronouncement of the death of God by a few of the more flamboyant secular theologians was a profession that radical Christianity is not really interested in theology at all. As in the Social Gospel, *man* is the central issue of secular theology. Religion must be humanized.

The radicals made more concrete the Neo-Orthodox notion of evangelism as the call for social action. They affirmed that social action *is* evangelism. Radical Christian thinkers also found useful, as a vague theological apparatus, the idea that God acts in history. For them, God is understood as a liberating force freeing men and women from political, economic, and social oppression. It is also clear in their thinking that God's will *can* be identified, roughly at least, with a specific program, not of reform, but of revolution. This program is generally interpreted as some kind of democratic or even Marxian socialism. If God is indeed active in the revolutionary social and political movements of our time, as the radical theologians claim, then Christians ought to be "where the action is." That is where theology ends and humanism takes over.

Until the mid-1960s, it may have been the case that the average layperson in the Liberal churches was not much concerned about even dramatic changes in the theological climate of America. But, when the historic denominations and Ecumenical structures began to take the radical stance seriously in their pronouncements and outlay of monies for what he or she considered questionable causes, the layperson finally rebelled, and so did many local congregations. Giving has either been curtailed or channeled away from the denominational and Ecumenical organizations which (1) do not represent the majority will of their constituencies and (2) make no solid attempt to demonstrate the relationship of what they are saying and doing to the Bible and biblical theology.

The average layperson in the churches of mainstream Ecumenical Liberalism has also become manifestly unhappy with the sermons he hears on Sunday and the instruction he receives in the church school classroom. No longer does he get answers to his ultimate questions of identity, meaning, and purpose. Where now is the authoritative word of the Lord once proclaimed from the pulpit and taught as an integral part of Christian education? And without the pastoral exhortation that he embrace a demanding moral and spiritual discipline—a "devout and holy life"—the layperson discerns nothing particularly distinctive about the Christian stance at all. So, given the current decline in this country of the social respectability attached to church membership in general and affiliation with certain denominations in particular, he now feels free either to look for another congregation where his religious needs *can* be met, or to forsake the institutional church altogether. Young people are especially apt to choose the latter option—to leave an institutional church which they view as the ecclesiastical manifestation of a shallow and hypocritical American Way of Life at best, and as a totally irrelevant religious form at worst. We can therefore say without qualification that mainstream Ecumenical Liberalism is in deep trouble. It may have won the war with Fundamentalism, but it has lost its soul in the process.

While Liberalism moved from the Social Gospel to Neo-Orthodoxy and back again to radical Christianity, Orthodoxy also underwent significant modification in both its Fundamentalist and Evangelical expressions. But, with its firm commitment to biblical authority and personal evangelism, Orthodox Christianity, unlike its Liberal counterpart, has enjoyed dramatic growth. Aided by the contemporary emphasis on internalization and experience, and supported by numerous defectors from Liberalism, Fundamentalism and Evangelicalism give every indication of becoming stronger in the future. Nevertheless, despite impressive numbers and prospects for continued growth, all is not well with modern Orthodoxy.

In their zeal to defend the faith against criticism, Fundamentalists and Evangelicals have given too many pat answers to profound questions. And by capitalizing on numerical strength, they have overlooked something very important about the Gospel. For if Liberals have reduced Christian faith to humanism, holders of the Orthodox position have been guilty of neglecting the social dimension of the Gospel entirely—seeking the salvation of souls but allowing bodies to go to hell. Fundamentalists and perhaps most Evangelicals have dismissed the biblical principle that faith without works is dead—that grace without discipleship is "cheap grace." They have too often ignored the fact that a new relationship with God in Jesus Christ calls for a new relationship with men and women. Orthodoxy has forgotten that Christian commitment, at its deepest level, is a narrow way not easily found—a path over which the disciple of Christ must always take up his cross. And history shows us that the way of the cross is never popular. In twentieth-century America, such action may result in persecution by the government and a pharisaic church when a Christian takes the side of the oppressed and in so doing prophetically challenges structured social evils (Matthew 5:11,12).

The Fundamentalist–Modernist controversy, as we have seen, has divided Protestant Christianity in America more deeply than ever before. Three warring factions have emerged—Liberalism, Fundamentalism, and Evangelicalism—each with its own ideological axe to grind. But to demonstrate that Evangelical Christianity is, in some measure at least, a vigorous attempt to maintain and renew the spirit of the New Testament and the primitive church in a secular age, we must now determine to what degree the various manifestations of contemporary Orthodoxy, as groups and individuals, are taking seriously the mandate for spiritual renewal by promoting reconciliation among belligerent Christians and by translating the imperatives of faith into concrete action.

II. The New Evangelical Orthodoxy

A. SCHOOLS OF ORTHODOXY

In the aftermath of the Fundamentalist–Modernist controversy, two dominant streams of Orthodoxy have come to the fore within American Christianity: Fundamentalism and Evangelicalism. Both schools of thought share a belief in the inspiration and authority of the Bible as the Word of God written, the indispensability of conversion, and the consequent need for traditional evangelism. Subtle variations in interpretation notwithstanding, both likewise give assent to what have become the five fundamentals of the faith—the virgin birth of Jesus Christ, his substitutionary atonement for man's sin, his bodily resurrection from the dead, and his literal and imminent Second Coming in glory, together with the aforementioned authority and inspiration of Scripture. Yet, taken as a whole, Fundamentalism differs from Evangelicalism dramatically in its basic attitudes. These are vividly discerned by Evangelical apologist Edward John Carnell, again in *The Case for Biblical Christianity*, when he describes the Fundamentalist posture as embracing "the quest for negative status, the elevation of minor issues to a place of major importance, the use of social mores as a norm of virtue, the toleration of one's own prejudices but not the prejudices of others, the confusion of the church with a denomination, and the avoidance of prophetic scrutiny by using the Word of God as an instrument of self-security but not self-criticism" (pp. 169—70).

Carnell also suggests that Fundamentalism tends to draw its followers chiefly from two sources. First, it attracts those who enjoy going it alone —who are separatists by nature. These people have little or no concern for the state of the Church universal. Second, Fundamentalism appeals to those whose theological and cultural attitudes have been shaped almost exclusively by the negativism of the Fundamentalist–Modernist Controversy. They find refuge in an ideology that sees only apostasy in the historic denominations. And while such persons may *outwardly* defend the Church universal, they do very little or nothing of a practical nature to translate that supposed affection into a program of outreaching fellowship.

For too long it has been the fault of mainstream Ecumenical Liberalism to lump together with pejorative intent *all* theological conservatives into the worn Fundamentalist category. In general, Evangelicals resent being called Fundamentalists, and Fundamentalists likewise do not usually appreciate the Evangelical designation. Moreover, since Carnell's remarks in 1959 and 1960, contrasting Fundamentalism with Evangelicalism (cultic Orthodoxy with classical Orthodoxy, as he termed them respectively), the issue has been further complicated by the emergence of several distinctive ideological subgroups within both schools of thought. This does not mean that the basic character of either Evangelicalism or Fundamentalism has changed. It merely indicates that both varieties of Orthodox Christianity have undergone modification to some degree in the finer points of theology and, more profoundly, in their attitudes toward culture.

1. Separatist Fundamentalism

Among the various expressions of Orthodoxy in America, *Separatist Fundamentalists* make up the most conservative ideological subgroup— theologically and otherwise. They are the direct descendants of those individuals and groups in the Fundamentalist–Modernist controversy who felt it necessary to separate *completely* from any manifestation of

Liberalism or Modernism they could discern. Characteristically, these Fundamentalists have also taken on an extreme and activist form of political and social conservatism, and it is often difficult to distinguish their theological concerns from the social and political stance they profess.

Contemporary Fundamentalist ideology is strongly reminiscent of the brazen and unmannerly revivalism typical of Billy Sunday (1862–1935), the professional baseball-player-turned-evangelist, who rode to fame on the crest of reaction against Social Gospel Liberalism. His "muscular" Christianity equated salvation with manliness and decency. Capitalizing on the excitement of World War I, Sunday then transformed masculine Christianity into "100 percent Americanism" which insisted that patriotism and Christianity are equivalent terms in the same way that "hell and traitors are synonymous." It was not long before he was attributing German atrocities to the influence of higher criticism on the German people. And when labor unrest appeared at the end of the war, the popular revivalist was quick to denounce foreign-inspired, godless social radicalism.

In the years immediately following World War I, the American people were hardly ready for any further tampering with the social order; so it became easy to demonstrate to the satisfaction of many that theological Liberalism or Modernism and communism were really reverse sides of the same coin. Thus the groundwork was provided for the rise of Christian anticommunism which was to become an integral part of the ideology of Separatist Fundamentalism in the course of its development.

With respect to theology, strictly speaking, the Separatist Fundamentalists, of course, are firmly committed to the five fundamentals of the faith. But their most cherished doctrines seem to be (1) total separation from ungodliness—especially its manifestations in Liberalism and Evangelicalism—as we have seen, (2) the verbal inspiration and inerrancy of the Bible, and (3) premillennial (and generally Dispensational) apocalypticism.

Separatist Fundamentalism tends to accept as a working doctrine the "dictation method" of biblical inspiration—the application of God's special guidance even to the choice of words in Scripture. This suggests that the writers were merely acting as stenographers without so much as contributing their own literary styles to the text. Judging modern English translations of the Bible as having been undertaken in large part by apostate scholars and their Evangelical cohorts, most Separatist Fundamentalists are quite content with the King James Version (1611) and regard it alone as sacred.

Influenced strongly by Dispensational theology, Separatist Fundamentalism holds an extremely pessimistic view of the present world situation. Its adherents see human society crumbling fast into decadence, old standards being swept away, loyalty to pure doctrine being scoffed at, and Satan reigning supreme throughout Christendom. Apostasy is everywhere. Those posing as Christians are destroying the faith of our fathers, say the Separatist Fundamentalists. Apostates are to be found in all areas of human activity—in colleges, seminaries, local churches, denominational and Ecumenical structures, among rich and poor, highly educated and unlearned alike. This predicament *proves* to Separatist Fundamentalists that the Last Days mentioned in the Bible have indeed arrived. Like other Dispensationalists, they understand biblical prophecy according to the timetable of dispensations suggested by scholars such as Darby and Scofield, and likewise accept only the literal interpretation of prophetic utterances in Scripture. So, by and large, Separatist Fundamentalism looks forward to (1) the imminent *rapture* of the Church (its being lifted into the skies to meet Christ and thence to heaven); followed in succession by (2) the earthly rule of Antichrist during the seven-year Great Tribulation; (3) the battle of Armageddon; (4) the millennial reign of Christ on earth; (5) another brief time of woes and Satan's rule over the world; and finally, the great white throne judgment in which the Devil and the damned are cast into a lake of everlasting and literal fire, while the righteous are rewarded by eternal bliss in a heaven that includes only Separatist Fundamentalists. For them, Jesus will have to wait to be Lord.

In Separatist Fundamentalism, theology is, practically speaking, less important than conservative political action. But in the context of Dispensational ideology, politics is a losing battle. No matter what specific political or social gains Separatist Fundamentalists might achieve by their noisy efforts, the decadence characteristic of the Last Days *must* get worse until the rapture, when the saved will finally be removed from this ever more sinful world. That is the message inherent in Dispensationalism; but Separatist Fundamentalists continue to fight for the status quo, the Protestant ethic and the morality implicit in Americanism, including militarism.

With respect to personal ethics (there is no social ethic) in Separatist Fundamentalism, negativism prevails. Cultural taboos are applied rigorously in the fight against worldliness which is looked upon as the fruit of apostasy—no drinking, no smoking, no social dancing, no gambling, no attendance at the theater, and the like. Righteous external behavior is emphasized, but it is interesting to note that the whole question of meaningful interpersonal relationships is bypassed in Separatist Fundamentalism except as it pertains to (1) separation from the ungodly and (2) submission to "legitimate" authority. Ethics has nothing to do with how a committed Christian treats other people as persons created in the image of God and for whom Christ died. And human love—not to mention Christ's love—appears to have no real importance in that school of thought.

The most significant groups, individuals and institutions representative of Separatist Fundamentalism are well known. They include the notorious Bob Jones University in Greenville, South Carolina, clearly the "world's most unusual university," as its catalog suggests; Major Edgar Bundy's Church League of America in Wheaton, Illinois; Dr. Fred Schwarz's Christian Anti-Communism Crusade, with headquarters in Long Beach, California; William Steuart McBirnie's "Voice of Americanism," Glendale, California; and most notably, Billy James Hargis's Christian Crusade in Tulsa, Oklahoma; and Carl McIntire's Twentieth Century Reformation movement, based in Collingswood, New Jersey, and his International Council of Christian Churches.

Billy James Hargis is an ordained minister in the Christian Church (Churches of Christ). Brought up in a poverty-stricken, Fundamentalist home in the South, Hargis had but one and one-half years of higher education before entering the ministry. In 1947, at the age of twenty-two, he decided to dedicate his life to the fight against communism, and in the years following, worked out a creed combining Americanism, free enterprise and Separatist Fundamentalism. Through Hargis's dynamic appeal, Christian Crusade grew from a local effort into an important national organization which includes American Christian College in Tulsa, a radio and television ministry that blankets the nation, a weekly newspaper with circulation in excess of 120,000, a publishing concern, and a resort hotel in Manitou Springs, Colorado, used as a conservative Christian conference center. Much has been made of Hargis's personal friendship with Rhodesia's Prime Minister Ian Smith, and his admiration for the government of the Republic of South Africa.

Although he practices separation from non-Fundamentalists in principle, Hargis recently accepted legal aid from, of all organizations, the National Council of Churches (NCC). In 1966, the founder of Christian Crusade lost his tax-exempt status for alleged political activities. He later won his case in a U.S. district court in 1971, but the favorable decision was overruled by the Tenth Circuit Court of Appeals in Denver in 1972. In an unsuccessful attempt to have the U.S. Supreme Court hear his appeal, the NCC provided him with its attorneys for the case. Obviously, the NCC in no way condones Hargis's theological, social, and political stance; but it *is* concerned that churches and other religious bodies (including itself) have the right to speak out on legislative issues without losing their tax-exempt status.

Carl McIntire, born in the Midwest in 1906, began his graduate training in theology at Princeton Theological Seminary, where he became a disciple of J. Greham Machen. When Machen broke with Princeton in 1929 to found Westminister Theological Seminary, McIntire went with him. Both were later dismissed from the ministry of the Presbyterian Church in 1936 for insubordination. During the same year, they organized a new denominational structure which was to become the Orthodox Presbyterian church. But, after Machen's death very early in 1937, McIntire formed yet another denomination on more separatist grounds, the Bible Presbyterian Church, and his own Faith Theological Seminary, now in Elkins Park, Pennsylvania. In 1941, he founded the American Council of Christian Churches (ACCC) and in 1948, the International Council of Christian Churches (ICCC) as conservative counterparts to the NCC and World Council of Churches (WCC) respectively. Both the ICCC and ACCC, however, are weak and internally fragmented organizations of small Separatist Fundamentalist denominations and churches.

McIntire has his own Bible Presbyterian congregation in Collingswood, New Jersey, where he originates a radio broadcast he claims is heard on over 500 stations coast to coast, and publishes a weekly newspaper, *Christian Beacon*, which regularly attacks Evangelicals and Liberals alike. In 1963, the radio preacher purchased a resort hotel in Cape May, New Jersey, and renamed it the Christian Admiral for use as a conservative conference center. Having lost his fight in New Jersey to regain state accreditation for Shelton College, a small liberal arts college he controls, McIntire moved it to a recently acquired major resort complex in Cape Canaveral, Florida, where he is also planning a freedom center to attract tourists and conference visitors from all over the nation and world.

Carl McIntire's message seems to become more extreme the older he gets. The radio preacher continues to denounce vigorously the NCC and WCC, the Roman Catholic Church, the Revised Standard Version (RSV) of the Bible, civil rights and antimilitarist legislation, foreign aid, alternative life-styles and, most of all, communism, against which he organized victory rallies in various American cities toward the end of U.S. military involvement in Indochina. But because his own ideological associates became increasingly resentful of McIntire's dictatorial conduct (something that has happened frequently before), he lost control of the ACCC, initially in 1968 and finally in 1970. Another personal defeat for McIntire came recently when the U.S. Supreme Court refused to hear an appeal that he be allowed to continue operation of WXUR, his suburban Philadelphia anchor station silenced in a bout with the Federal Communications Commission over its "Fairness Doctrine" regulating the broadcasting of controversial political issues. McIntyre then purchased an old World War II minesweeper and anchored it beyond the three-mile limit off Cape May, hoping to run a pirate radio station he calls "Radio Free America." But the legality of such an operation is in doubt, and the FCC clearly intends to torpedo this station as well. Furthermore, the radio preacher's son, Carl Thomas, once head of the ICCC's International Christian Youth and possible successor to his father, has now become a self-styled "radical Christian" and teaches at the Institute for Christian Studies (an Evangelical institution) in Toronto, Canada. So, the elder McIntire's influence in this country, at least, appears to be on the wane. And the question remains as to who will lead the Twentieth Century Reformation movement once the forceful radio preacher himself passes from the scene.

If Carl McIntire is perhaps even more separatist in his ideology than Billy James Hargis, it must be noted that the former has at the same time been most anxious to meet and "fellowship" with various world political leaders of conservative persuasion who can hardly be termed Fundamentalists. These personalities include both General Ky, a Buddhist, and President Thieu, a Buddhist turned Roman Catholic, of South Vietnam. Such a fact merely demonstrates the point that McIntire, like other Separatist Fundamentalists, is clearly as interested in ultraconservative politics as in theology.

The presidential campaign of 1964 gave the Separatist Fundamentalists a golden opportunity to promote their cause among the American people at large. Aligning themselves in no uncertain terms with the candidacy of Barry Goldwater, they were vigorous workers in the campaign, especially in their distribution of fear-instilling and grossly exaggerated books like John Stormer's *None Dare Call It Treason* and their widespread use of the media for other propaganda. Separatist Fundamentalists took the line that the election of Goldwater as president of the United States was the last chance for America to prevent a communist takeover. Many seemingly believed their ludicrous assertion. But when Goldwater was defeated by a landslide, and the communist takeover still did not materialize, Separatist Fundamentalism suffered a devastating blow. Its grim predictions did not come to pass, and no longer did it have a *practical* program the support of which might actually bring its goals to pass. Hence, since the end of 1964, Separatist Fundamentalism and the radical right as a whole have begun to lose the popularity they once enjoyed.

If we are looking for an expression of Orthodox Christianity genuinely concerned about spiritual renewal and the wholeness of the Gospel, we shall have to search elsewhere. Separatist Fundamentalism, with its Dispensational pessimism about the human situation, its firm commitment to the political and social status quo, its anti-intellectualism heightened by an inherent refusal to be self-critical or to compromise, and its ideology of separatism, has nothing to offer in this regard. That school of theology takes pride in the divison among Christians and glorifies the "virtue of selfishness." Separatist Fundamentalism is totally destitute of a social conscience.

2. Open Fundamentalism

As a manifestation of contemporary Orthodoxy, *Open Fundamentalism* is less easily identified and defined than Separatist Fundamentalism.

Both schools of thought are Dispensationalist and hold to a strictly literal interpretation of Scripture, including the Genesis account of creation. Both adhere to the five fundamentals of the faith and espouse a generally negative personal morality. But Open Fundamentalism repudiates the explicit alliance of Fundamentalism with ultraconservative politics in the belief that the religious and political spheres ought to be separate. Nevertheless, given its strong Dispensational outlook, Open Fundamentalism tends to support the conservative and anticommunist position on most social and political issues. Like Separatist Fundamentalism, it too holds to a basic separatism from the historic denominations and their "unbelieving" theologians and ministers. Yet, Open Fundamentalism is less vocal and clearly less extreme about its separatist posture. And not inherently anti-intellectual, it is also quite often willing to engage in dialogue with other Orthodox schools of thought, at least, and is capable of some measure of self-criticism.

As the direct descendant of the Bible-school movement in America, Open Fundamentalism owes much to the thinking of Dispensational theologians such as Reuben Archer Torrey, C. I. Scofield, Lewis Sperry Chafer, H. A. Ironside, and more recently, Charles C. Ryrie, Dwight Pentecost, and John F. Walvoord. It is best represented by various smaller denominations (including Pentecostal bodies), by the large number of independent, nondenominational Bible churches, and by the more conservative elements of the Jesus People. Intellectual centers of Open Fundamentalism include the Moody Bible Institute in Chicago, Talbot Theological Seminary in La Mirada, California (an outgrowth of the old Bible Institute of Los Angeles), and most of all, Dallas Theological Seminary. Unlike Separatist Fundamentalism, Open Fundamentalism seeks to maintain an academic respectability for its Dispensational ideology by the frequent production of scholarly works on the topic, including the journal, *Bibliotheca Sacra*, now published by Dallas Theological Seminary, a graduate school of theology which requires four years of study (rather than three) for its first professional degree and an extensive grounding in both Greek and Hebrew for all students.

Although Open Fundamentalism sympathizes with the Evangelical desire to escape the odium surrounding the *Fundamentalist* designation, it sees no reason to abandon the term completely. John F. Walvoord, president of Dallas Theological Seminary, does not find in Evangelicalism any attempt to escape the fundamentals of the faith. But he prefers the Fundamentalist name, since it carries a "clear, historical and theological meaning, while the term *evangelical* lends itself to manipulation by the modern liberal confusing both laity and clergy."[1] Nevertheless, a sizable number of characteristically Open Fundamentalist denominations and independent churches *are* members of the National Association of Evangelicals and support Evangelical causes, most notably the efforts of Billy Graham.

A good example of popular Open Fundamentalist thought is Hal Lindsey's phenomenal bestseller, *The Late Great Planet Earth*, and its sequel, *Satan Is Alive and Well on Planet Earth*. In these journalese studies, Lindsey presents a popularization of traditional Dispensational theology. Relating current political events and examples of social change on the world scene to Dispensational expectations, he talks about the increasing social decadence of the Last Days, the mounting apostasy in the historic denominations, and the trend toward a world government controlled, ultimately, by Satan during the seven-year Great Tribulation period.

Lindsey, a graduate of Dallas Theological Seminary, was once director of Campus Crusade for Christ at the University of California, Los Angeles (UCLA), but broke with that group in the mid-1960s to found his own ministry to students near the UCLA campus—the Jesus Christ Light and Power Company. Apparently disenchanted by the Campus Crusade bureaucracy, its rigid evangelistic approach and cultural demands, Lindsey identified himself with the emerging Jesus People and Charismatic Renewal. His belief in the apostate nature of the historic denominations allows him to sympathize with the revolt of young people against the institutional church and its doctrinally "polluted" and culturally determined structures. In this connection, Lindsey also seems to condone the youthful search for an alternative Christian life-style; although he himself, as the result of the success of his books, lives in fashionable Pacific Palisades, California, and has recently moved his office to the equally prestigious Century City district of Los Angeles.

If Open Fundamentalism is indeed a more moderate expression of Orthodox Christianity than Separatist Fundamentalism, it too offers very little or nothing to the contemporary search for spiritual renewal. The unyielding Dispensational view of the present human situation which characterizes Open Fundamentalism deprives it of a meaningful social ethic. And its basic ideology of separatism prevents that school of theology from viewing positively any plan or program for reconciliation among Christians.

3. Establishment Evangelicalism

As we have seen, a group of young theologians emerged during the 1940s in reaction to the obscurantism, anti-intellectualism and bad manners so characteristic of what Fundamentalism had been up until then. These Orthodox scholars were joined by clergy and laymen alike in the formation of the National Association of Evangelicals. Their choice of the designation *Evangelical* bears witness to the fact that they considered evangelism or proclaiming the good news their primary concern.

In the course of the years since the 1940s, the Neo-Evangelicals have been joined by the Billy Graham Evangelistic Association and a host of other organizations dedicated to the cause of proclaiming the message of Jesus Christ throughout the world—calling men and women to repentance and belief in the Gospel. Their cause has been further advanced by the founding of *Christianity Today* as a highly successful platform of Evangelical thought, and by the marked growth and increasing academic respectability of Evangelical colleges and seminaries. In fact, it is now quite possible to talk about Evangelicalism as *the* established expression of Orthodoxy in the United States, if not the world.

Although considerable diversity of thinking is found within its ranks, the Evangelical countermovement to mainstream Ecumenical Liberalism is, by and large, "committed to giving meticulous and sharp study to the words of Scripture, the definitions of theology, the absolutes of ethics, and the differentia of the churches."[2] Like Fundamentalism, *Establishment Evangelicalism* adheres to the inspiration and authority of the Bible. But it does not limit itself to the *literal* interpretation of Scripture at all points, nor does it revere any particular translation. Furthermore, among Establishment Evangelicals, the whole question of the *nature* of biblical authority and inspiration has been reopened. And despite the fact that a good number of Establishment Evangelicals still hold a basic Dispensational view of history, there is a discernible trend away from Dispensationalism as a tool for interpreting the Bible. Their acceptance of the reliability and normative character of Scripture gives Establishment Evangelicals a solid basis from which to maintain precision in theological investigation and to determine divinely revealed ethical absolutes. In this way, they differ markedly from mainstream Ecumenical Liberals who tend to reduce theology to ethics, and ethics to the one norm of *love* which is not precisely defined, since Liberalism has no propositional authority (in the Bible) from which to proceed. Establishment Evangelicalism has always professed to have a social conscience and a biblically based social ethic. But its social concern has most often been characterized by caution at best and inaction or reaction at worst. Finally, unlike the Fundamentalists, Establishment Evangelicals do not espouse a separatist stance. They are open both to dialogue and some forms of cooperation with other schools of thought. Nevertheless, Establishment Evangelicals generally favor the search for spiritual rather than institutional Christian unity, believing that there can be no meaningful solidarity apart from basic doctrinal agreement.

Establishment Evangelicalism is represented by denominations that are members of the National Association of Evangelicals (NAE)—such as the Baptist General Conference, Christian and Missionary Alliance, Conservative Congregational Christian Conference, Evangelical Free Church of America, and Free Methodist Church. It is typified by independent churches and by congregations from nonaligned denominations—such as the Christian Reformed Church, Church of the Nazarene, Churches of Christ, Conservative Baptist Association, Evangelical Covenant Church, and Grace Brethren Churches—which belong to the NAE individually. Establishment Evangelicalism also embraces the greater bulk of membership within both the Southern Baptist Convention and the Lutheran Church, Missouri Synod, neither of which is a constituent member of the NAE or the NCC–WCC. In addition, it is representative of individual churches related to the NAE whose denominations are members of the NCC–WCC. These congregations come from the American Baptist Churches, Presbyterian Church in the U.S., Reformed Church in America, United Methodist Church, and United Presbyterian Church in the USA. Finally, Establishment Evangelicalism is a stance held by small to large contingents within most of the Ecumenically aligned denominations apart from any separate affiliation with the NAE.

Intellectual centers of Establishment Evangelicalism include Wheaton College in Illinois (the "Evangelical Harvard," which has graduated such eminent Evangelical leaders as Billy Graham, Leighton Ford, Carl Henry, Harold Lindsell, and the late Edward John Carnell) and Westmont College, Santa Barbara, California. Both are interdenominational and emphasize undergraduate education. Graduate schools of theology include Trinity Evangelical Divinity School, Deerfield, Illinois; Gordon-Conwell Theological Seminary, Wenham, Massachusetts; Asbury Theological Seminary, Wilmore, Kentucky; and the especially prominent Fuller Theological Seminary, Pasadena, California. Unlike most Fundamentalist seminaries, all are accredited by the American Association of Theological Schools and have high academic standards. Committed students from any denomination are considered for admission.

Very significant within Establishment Evangelicalism is the impressive number of independent, international organizations for evangelism both in America and abroad. Most notable, perhaps, are Youth for Christ, which engages in evangelistic activity among high school students, and Campus Crusade for Christ, an international ministry of evangelism to college and university students in particular and to laypersons in general.

Begun in 1951 as a ministry to students at UCLA, Campus Crusade for Christ was founded by businessman-turned-seminarian Bill Bright and his wife, with the help of the late Dr. Henrietta Mears, then Director of Christian Education at the First Presbyterian Church of Hollywood, California. Today, Crusade has a full-time staff of over 3000 in the United States and fifty other countries. Staff members are generally trained at the main multi-million-dollar headquarters (formerly a large resort hotel) in Arrowhead Springs, California. But Crusade also manages centers in Manila, London, Switzerland, and Mexico. Each full-time staff worker must raise his or her own support (ranging in 1972 from $285 monthly for a single person just beginning to about $950 for a staff member of long standing with four children—plus housing and auto allowance) and follow a tight discipline imposed by headquarters. Crusade operated on a $2 million annual budget in 1972, and has plans to reach a phenomenal $200 million annually by 1980. No longer exclusively a campus ministry, Crusade trains more than 100,000 people yearly in lay institutes of evangelism. And its special divisions work with pastors, missionaries, Blacks, Native Americans, Spanish-speaking people, and military personnel.

Central to the Campus Crusade for Christ message are its Four Spiritual Laws, developed by Bill Bright in his booklet, *Have You Heard of the Four Spiritual Laws?* These laws are viewed by Crusade as governing one's relationship with God:

1. God *loves* you, and has a wonderful *plan* for your life (John 3:16; 10:10).
2. Man is *sinful* and *separated* from God, thus he cannot know and experience God's love and plan for his life (Romans 3:23; 6:23).
3. Jesus Christ is God's *only* provision for man's sin. Through Him you can know and experience God's love and plan for your life (Romans 5:8; I Corinthians 15:3–6; John 14:6).
4. We must individually *receive* Jesus Christ as Savior and Lord; then we can know and experience God's love and plan for our lives (John 1:12; Ephesians 2:8, 9; Revelation 3:20).

After the Laws are presented to a prospective convert, he or she is invited immediately to receive Christ through a sincere prayer: "Lord Jesus, I need You. I open the door of my life and receive You as my Savior and Lord. Thank You for forgiving my sins. Take control of the throne of my life. Make me the kind of person You want me to be." The method of evangelism is simple. Behind it is a strong concern to train Christians to share their faith with their peers. First, a staff worker presents the Four Spiritual Laws to a potential convert, using the Bible for reference. Second, he or she presses for a decision. Third, the staff worker enrolls his or her new convert in a follow-up program. And fourth, the newly born-again Christian is urged to recruit others. Some Evangelical critics argue that Crusade's methods are too rash, anti-intellectual and simplistic. Theologians complain that the message is too narrow and devoid of a solid theological content. Many Evangelicals feel that Crusade has neglected the social dimension of the Gospel (although it *has* recently begun to consider social issues in the course of its evangelism). It is also clear that Campus Crusade for Christ might once have been more characteristic of Open Fundamentalism than Establishment Evangelicalism. Nevertheless, by its manifestly successful "Explo 72" evangelism conference held in Dallas, its participation in the inter-denominational evangelistic movement, "Key 73," and its discovery of social concern and apparent de-emphasis of cultural demands after conversion, Crusade now stands squarely within the Establishment Evangelical school of thought.

One organization, one personality, and one interdenominational journal of opinion together constitute the three most important symbols of Establishment Evangelicalism in America today. The National Association of Evangelicals, as we have seen, was formed in 1942 as a voluntary association of Protestant Evangelical denominations and churches who were unhappy about the Federal Council of Churches and its embracing of the Liberal theological and social stance. United by a commonly accepted Orthodox statement of faith, the NAE had among its members in 1972, thirty-four complete denominations and individual churches from twenty-six other denominations. Its headquarters are located in Wheaton, Illinois, but the NAE also has seven regional instrumentalities and an Office of Public Affairs in Washington, D.C., which is concerned primarily with the infringement of religious liberties. Eleven commissions and five affiliated service groups are part of the NAE as well. Most significant of these are, perhaps, the Evangelical Foreign Missions Association, serving fifty-eight member mission boards with some 6000 missionaries in 108 countries; the National Religious Broadcasters and Radio–TV Commission; the National Association of Christian Schools; and the National Sunday School Association. By the final article in its own statement of faith, the NAE as an organization, is charged with furthering the "spiritual unity" of *all* believers in Christ.

One original intent of the NAE was to provide a recognizable foundation through which to retake the historic denominations from the Liberals by persuasion from within rather than criticism from without. Yet, this goal has clearly not been achieved. Another reason for the formation of the NAE was to provide a meaningful fellowship among Evangelicals in cooperative witness. But, as a recent advertisement in *United Evangelical Action* (the official organ of the NAE) suggested, few Evangelicals even *know* about the organization's existence: "From all visible evidence, in the minds or hearts of millions of evangelicals, clergy and laity alike, NAE simply does not exist. It is not a presence to be dealt with. Not a group or cause. Not even a good idea."[3] In other words, despite the NAE's outspoken criticism of the search for Christian unity on the institutional level, it has been manifestly unsuccessful in *its* quest for an alternative spiritual unity—even among Evangelicals themselves. Finally, like Establishment Evangelicalism in general—and unlike Fundamentalist interdenominational associations—the NAE declares unequivocally that it does have a social conscience. But its Social Concern

Commission has done little more than coordinate various Evangelical social welfare agencies. Furthermore, the NAE's annual resolutions dealing with issues in the wider society can hardly be termed "prophetic." Typical of these are some of the pronouncements made in 1972: (1) Capital punishment should be retained for premeditated capital crimes; (2) Congress ought to award tax credit for gifts to institutions of higher learning; (3) Congress should enact legislation to prevent the use of alcoholic beverages aboard commercial airlines; and (4) Congress ought to enact legislation to restrict smoking to designated seats on commercial flights.

At any rate, despite its failure to be a viable force for unity among Evangelicals, its powerlessness as an instrument for outreach and reconciliation beyond the Evangelical community, and its inability to translate Orthodox faith into works as prophetic social action, the NAE remains the organizational symbol of Establishment Evangelicalism. It provides a national identification for Evangelicals.

More important than the NAE as a symbol of Establishment Evangelicalism, however, is one individual: Billy Graham. William Franklin Graham, Jr. graduated from Wheaton College with a degree in anthropology in 1943, and began his career shortly thereafter as an ordained Southern Baptist evangelist. In the wake of his early revival successes in 1949 and the following year, Graham launched his "Hour of Decision" radio broadcasts and formed the Billy Graham Evangelistic Association in Minneapolis during 1950. Given his dynamic style and handsome appearance, it is natural that the forceful evangelist would derive increasing benefit from regular exposure to the mass media. So today Billy Graham ranks among the most prominent personalities in the world.

Theologically speaking, Graham's message has not changed with the passage of time. He is still firmly committed in his determination to confront sinful men and women with the claims of Christ and bring them to the point of a personal decision for Jesus Christ as Savior and Lord. Billy Graham believes that only born-again individuals are adequately equipped to live truly meaningful lives and change society for the better in the process:

We have been trying to solve every ill of society as though society were made up of regenerate men to whom we had an obligation to speak with Christian

advice. . . . Thus the government may try to legislate Christian behavior, but
it soon finds that man remains unchanged.

The changing of men is the primary mission of the church. The only way to
change men is to get them converted to Jesus Christ. Then they will have the
capacity to live up to the Christian command to "Love thy neighbor."[4]

And although he has somewhat modified his original Dispensational
stance, Graham continues to be more or less pessimistic about the
contemporary human situation and sees ultimate improvement only
with the Second Coming of Christ.

If Evangelicals regard Billy Graham as the most effective mass evangelist in history, the average American looks at him as the embodiment
of all that is good in American life. Hence, it is not really his Evangelical
message that makes Graham the most admired person in America today;
it is what he represents. Lowell Streiker and Gerald Strober comment
on this point:"Graham, who through sincere introspection continues to
regard himself as evangelist called to witness to the saving knowledge
of Christ and the new birth, has transcended a purely theological ministry and has emerged as the spokesman not of preachers and Presidents
but of the political views of the corporate majority of Americans."[5]

Since the early days of his mass evangelism, Billy Graham *has* professed a strong social concern—despite his Dispensational outlook and
his emphasis on personal conversion. In the early days of the civil rights
movement, he took important symbolic action by refusing to speak to
segregated audiences here and abroad. He integrated his staff and spoke
in favor of the Civil Rights Act of 1964. Unlike most of his theological
constituency, Graham preferred Lyndon Johnson over Barry Goldwater
in the 1964 general election. Later he would give his blessing to Johnson's War on Poverty. Indeed, Billy Graham has written concerning his
social conscience: "Certainly we as Christian citizens have no right to
be content with our social order until the principles of Christ are applied
to all men. As long as there is enslaved one man who should be free,
as long as slums and ghettos exist, as long as any person goes to bed
hungry at night, as long as the color of a man's skin is his prison, there
must be a divine discontent."[6] But it seems to Graham's Liberal and
Evangelical critics that in recent years his role as a kind of unofficial
chaplain to presidents has been characterized more by the political
conservatism typical of Middle America rather than the prophetic social

concern he once professed to embrace. If mainstream Ecumenical Liberals in the past criticized Billy Graham for his appeal to the emotions (something few Liberals would do today), they now feel that he is wrong in neglecting a unique opportunity to influence the highest circles of political life for the cause of social righteousness. Liberals and some Evangelicals are increasingly disturbed by Graham's present disregard for the social dimension of the Gospel—which they view as one result of his Dispensational eschatology. The reaction of John Coleman Bennett (president emeritus of Union Theological Seminary) to the evangelist's Oakland, California, Crusade in 1971 is a case in point:

His eschatology enables him to chastise America without disturbing the particular *respectable* forms of power in our midst, especially those responsible for the use of power by our nation abroad. Graham does not have to have new directions of policy that would threaten them. Jesus will set things right on this level.

He can denounce war in general, corruption, the drug culture, the preoccupation with sex, racial discrimination, and all manifestations of greed, and yet what he says will not trouble the powers most responsible for these evils. . . .[7]

In the wake of much criticism from Liberal churchmen over his failure to condemn the president's bombing of Hanoi in December 1972, Billy Graham answered his critics. Denying his role as a White House "chaplain," Graham went on to say:

It has been my privilege to be acquainted with five Presidents during my ministry. While I have attempted to avoid issues which are strictly political, at the same time I have spoken and continue to speak on issues in which I feel a definite moral issue is involved. . . . I am convinced that God has called me to be a New Testament evangelist, not an Old Testament prophet! While some may interpret an evangelist to be primarily a social reformer or political activist, I do not! An evangelist is a proclaimer of the message of God's love and grace in Jesus Christ and the necessity of repentance and faith. . . . The people of the world need a new birth that only Christ can bring.[8]

In the same statement, the evangelist declared his abhorrence of war in general and offered his prayers for an early armistice in Vietnam. But, citing Matthew and James, he also asserted that "we will always have wars until the coming again of the Prince of Peace." Of particular significance regarding Graham's remarks, however, are his espousal of a vocation as a "New Testament evangelist" rather than an "Old Testament prophet," and his reiteration of the typical Evangelical position that changed individuals alone can bring about a transformed society. Thus Billy Graham functions well as the most eminent spokesman and representative symbol of contemporary Establishment Evangelicalism.

In 1956, a biweekly magazine was born to give Evangelical Christianity "a clear voice to speak with conviction and love, and to state its true position and its relevance to the world crisis."[9] Since then, *Christianity Today* has become *the* periodical voice of Establishment Evangelicalism, and like the NAE and Billy Graham, one of its most important symbols. A wide range of Evangelical opinion is to be found in each issue of the magazine, but, as it stated in the same editorial, "Those who direct the editorial policy of *Christianity Today* unreservedly accept the complete reliability and authority of the written Word of God. It is their conviction that the Scriptures teach the doctrine of plenary inspiration."

Christianity Today has effectively demonstrated that the Evangelical stance is not inherently anti-intellectual. Carl Henry, the journal's first editor, is a polished and scholarly spokesman for Orthodoxy. The magazine's present editor and publisher, Harold Lindsell, is also an articulate academician in his own right. *Christianity Today*'s high-caliber essays deal with every aspect of theology, and its coverage of religious news throughout the world has been hailed by Evangelical and Liberal alike. Although the periodical's Ecumenical counterparts, *Christianity and Crisis* and *The Christian Century*, seem to have forsaken basic theological concerns for politics, *Christianity Today* is still attempting to discover a solid biblical-theological foundation for action in the world—even if its conclusions generally turn out conservative. Like Establishment Evangelicalism as a whole, *Christianity Today* admits the necessity of Christian social concern. But *caution* is the byword in its editorial comments. And for this journal of Evangelical opinion, social action must always be subordinate to personal salvation, as a recent leading editorial clearly maintains:

The Church should lay down biblical principles for a just society from Scripture, and it should train its people to do their job as citizens of Caesar's kingdom to bring about needed social change. But while the Church is to be concerned about temporal power struggles, its first and ultimate interest lies in the spiritual struggle with the powers of darkness. The watchword is . . . salvation, the reconciling of man to God by faith in Jesus Christ through Christ's blood sacrifice on Calvary.[10]

In Establishment Evangelicalism, we have discerned an honest effort to break away from the separatist impulse and social unconcern of Fundamentalism. The endeavors of those who first called themselves Evangelicals are worthy of praise in this respect. But we have also seen that Establishment Evangelicalism's rejection of separatism in principle has not led to a meaningful outreach to Christians of other persuasions, nor has it brought about any *significant* unity (institutional *or* spiritual) within a deeply divided Christendom. Furthermore, we have found social concern among Establishment Evangelicals to be often merely an offering of pious words rather than a demonstration of prophetic action. Hence, if we are looking for a powerful expression of spiritual renewal in Orthodox Christianity—one genuinely committed to reconciliation and active faith in a secular society—we shall have to search elsewhere.

4. The New Evangelicalism

Donald Bloesch, professor of theology at Dubuque Theological Seminary, has noticed some important trends in the school of thought we have designated Establishment Evangelicalism. As a result of this intellectual transformation within respectable Orthodoxy, he calls the developing mood the *New Evangelicalism* as a movement wider and deeper than the original Neo-Evangelicalism which has now become Establishment Evangelicalism. The new Orthodox theology is being manifested in the leading Evangelical seminaries and in other circles of Evangelical thought both in the United States and Europe.

First, there is emerging a fresh understanding of the reliability and authority of Scripture. The New Evangelicals are firm in their acceptance of the principle of historical criticism. They acknowledge that the Bible is the word of man as well as the Word of God, since the divine Word is made known by means of a human word, bearing the marks of cultural conditioning. The old concepts of infallibility and inerrancy are being reinterpreted to the point that a number of Evangelical scholars are saying that the *teaching* of Scripture (i.e., matters of faith and practice) rather than the text itself is without error. Furthermore, the flawless message of the Bible is viewed as available to man *only* through the working of the Holy Spirit. But the New Evangelicals insist at the same time that the revealed Word of God, Jesus Christ, must never be set against the written Word (as in Neo-Orthodoxy) which remains the definitive witness to Christ. Inspiration, then, still plays a significant role in New Evangelical thought, even though its scholars clearly reject any mechanical theory of inspiration that would detract from the humanity of the biblical authors. And it is increasingly the case that the former are beginning to discern God's revelation both in the words of Scripture *and* in the historical events recorded therein.

Second, the New Evangelicals are again emphasizing the necessity of meaningful sanctification following regeneration (or the new birth). For them, it is not enough merely to be pardoned of sin; one must also be *cleansed* from sin and adequately equipped thereby to live a new life. The life in Christ, moreover, is seen to be just as important as correct doctrine. And while legalism and moralism are censured unequivocally, there is a mounting interest among the New Evangelicals in the "social holiness" characteristic of John Wesley. In a word, Christian practice is to be understood as the *indispensable* consequence or fruit of a dynamic faith.

Third, there is in the New Evangelicalism a marked aversion to Dispensationalism and its inherent apocalyptic speculations. This firm repudiation, of course, frees the scholars in question to deal more constructively with the present ills of society and thus develop a positive Evangelical social ethic, unhindered by Dispensational pessimism concerning the human situation.

Fourth, the New Evangelicals are, in fact, displaying a fresh interest in the social dimension of the Gospel. Their emphasis is still on spiritual rebirth, but a strong effort is being made to relate the inward change of heart to the demands of a more righteous society. For them, individual conversion is the precondition for revolutionary social transformation, yet conversion *by itself* is not enough to bring about such change. It must be supplemented by a practical social involvement together with all men and women of good will. In this connection, the New Evangelicals hold a refreshingly optimistic theology grounded not in the innate moral possibilities within man himself but in the corporeal resurrection of Jesus Christ and the mystery of a new birth which begins in the here and now. Among these scholars there is a feeling that the ideal of sainthood can be partially realized in the historical present if Christians are willing to reassert the prophetic dimension of their faith. Evangelicalism has become too closely identified with the bourgeois class and the status quo. The New Evangelicals are calling it to reject this identification and so rediscover the radicalism inherent in authentic Christian faith.

Fifth, the New Evangelicalism has reopened dialogue with mainstream Ecumenical Liberalism and has begun to converse with representatives of other religious traditions and even with Marxists:

Evangelical ecumenism aims for the reconciliation of the various churches and the separated brethren but not necessarily organic union. It sees dialogue not as a means to arrive at the truth but to clarify and illumine the truth. It regards conversations with Marxists and other religions as a means of furthering the proclamation of the gospel instead of forging a new cultural synthesis in which the Christian message would be drastically diluted.[11]

Bloesch also mentions other interesting but perhaps less important characteristics of the New Evangelicalism. He does, however, omit one especially significant trend within this stream of thought. And that is the increasing friendliness between Evangelical Christianity and science. As long ago as the 1940s and 50s, Evangelical scholars such as Edward John Carnell and Bernard Ramm were espousing theories of theistic evolution seemingly more compatible with the findings of biology and geology than the traditional creationist view had been. In the years following, much debate has taken place within Evangelical circles on the matter. But in the wake of the present decline of a literalist Dispensational perspective in Evangelical scholarship, mounting acceptance of theistic evolution in some form has become noticeable. At least, it is obvious that most Evangelical theologians have turned their attention to apparently more crucial issues.

If the New Evangelicalism is a very important stance within Orthodoxy in its own right, it is even more notable for its influence on an emerging generation of college and university students, recent seminary graduates, "street people," intellectuals, activists, pastors, evangelists, politicians, and concerned laypersons in general, all of whom we shall call the Young Evangelicals. Although the views held by these individuals are often indistinguishable from those espoused by New Evangelical thinkers like Clarence Bass, Vernon Grounds, George Ladd, David Moberg, J. Rodman Williams, and the immortal Edward John Carnell, the Young Evangelical stance might be described more appropriately as a "spirit" rather than a well-defined theology. Furthermore, it would be improper to imply that all the Young Evangelicals are physically youthful. Indeed, some are not. But whether young or old, they are *all* characterized by (1) a fresh spirit of openness to all who seek to follow Jesus Christ and (2) a profound desire to apply the Gospel to *every* dimension of life. Most of the Young Evangelicals are aware of the Fundamentalist–Modernist controversy only from their studies; they display none of the theological and cultural prejudices so vividly manifested in that debate and its aftermath. They have no axe to grind. And their older compatriots who share the same spirit also have firmly and completely rejected the separatist impulse, the bad manners as well as the social unconcern rightly associated with the Fundamentalist position.

Rooted in biblical Orthodoxy and its most dynamic contemporary expressions, the Young Evangelicals have been motivated on the one hand by the concerns of the New Evangelicalism, and on the other hand by the conscience-rending social and political unrest of the 1960s—the civil rights struggle, the tragedy of Indochina, the student rights movement, the ecology movement, the increasingly visible generation gap, the decline of the historic denominations, the hypocrisy of the Evangelical churches, and the worldwide cry for liberation. Carl Henry has astutely discerned a number of things the Young Evangelicals expect from their churches:

1. An interest in human beings not simply as souls to be saved but as whole persons;

2. More active involvement by evangelical Christians in sociopolitical affairs;

3. An honest look at many churches' idolatry of nationalism;

4. Adoption of new forms of worship;

5. An end to judging spiritual commitment by such externals as dress, hair style and other participation in cultural trends, including rock music;

6. A new spirit with regard to ecumenical or nonecumenical attitudes;

7. Bold and, if need be, costly involvement in the revolutionary struggles of our day; and finally,

8. A reappraisal of life values.[12]

The Young Evangelicals are coming to see that the standard conservative assault on the Social Gospel is often merely a convenient excuse to avoid the imperatives of practical Christian service. At the same time, they are also discovering that Christian faith cannot rightly be identified with any single religious style or with a particular political or economic philosophy, be it laissez-faire or Marxist. The Young Evangelicals fault Establishment Evangelicalism for too often exhibiting the Fundamentalist sentiments it says it disdains, for its de facto separatism, and for its failure to implement its avowed (or supposed) social concern into concrete sacrificial action.

Unlike Separatist and Open Fundamentalism, and unlike Establishment Evangelicalism as well, the Young Evangelicals, supported by the thinking of the New Evangelicals, demonstrate a genuine spirit of renewal in Orthodox Christianity. Once more, their uncompromising bent on reconciliation among Christians and on prophetic action in the world is evidence of something even more than renewal. The Young Evangelicals, as individuals and groups, represent nothing less than a *revolution* in Orthodoxy. For this reason, we shall take a closer look at who these people are and what they are doing later in our discussion.

B. CHARISMATIC RENEWAL

In treating the four major ideological subgroups of Orthodox Christianity in America today, we have thus far omitted one important school of thought, because it does not fit neatly either in the Fundamentalist or Evangelical designation. *Charismatic Renewal* or *Neo-Pentecostalism* is an enthusiastic, very experiential manifestation of basic Orthodoxy that includes not only Fundamentalists, Evangelicals, and mainstream Ecumenical Liberals, but also Roman Catholics, who find their unity more in experience than in doctrine.

In principle, Charismatic Renewal is a transdenominational if not

Ecumenical movement which emerged and became recognizable in the historic denominations only in 1960. It is theologically diverse but generally Orthodox, and is unified by a common experience—the Baptism of the Holy Spirit—with accompanying *charismata* or spiritual gifts to be used personally and corporately in the life of the Church. Evangelical and conversionist, the movement is also genuinely reformist in character, and is represented largely by persons from the middle and upper-middle socioeconomic levels of society. These attributes, since they indicate a radical departure from the sectarianism and separatism usually associated with the (denominational) Pentecostal movement as a whole, are highly significant.

Roman Catholics, Anglicans, Eastern Orthodox Christians, and Protestants of most historic and exclusively Evangelical denominations (and a few Open Fundamentalist churches) are included. The Pentecostal or Charismatic experience is understood to transcend denominational and ideological walls while at the same time it clarifies and underscores what is authentically Christian in each tradition without demanding structural or even doctrinal changes in any given church body.

Charismatic Renewal is Ecumenical, though not in the sense that it openly seeks institutional unity as a goal. Michael Harper, one-time curate under John R. W. Stott at All Souls Church, Langham Place, London, is now editor of *Renewal* and director of the Fountain Trust in London, Great Britain's most important Neo-Pentecostal Organization. He stresses that the movement is more concerned with *spiritual* unity at the grass roots level than with organic union engineered by Ecumenical planners:

There is a sharing together at the deep levels of worship, prayer, spiritual gifts and ministries and testimony, as well as biblical teaching. This is not to disguise the fact that there are still many differences between Christians and many difficulties in the pathway to unity. But those involved believe that this is where Christians should *begin* in their quest for unity, not at the conference table or the debating chamber. . . . The ecumenical movement seems to put the cart before the horse; whereas this new move of the Holy Spirit is indicating what we should be doing first.[13]

Nevertheless, Neo-Pentecostalism is generally friendly in its attitude toward the Ecumenical structures such as the World Council of

Churches and its regional counterparts. Furthermore, the Protestant–Roman Catholic encounter within Charismatic Renewal is so intense and heartfelt that it is probably unparalleled in contemporary ecclesiastical experience. In view of this fact, Harper again asserts in *None Can Guess* "that this movement is the most unifying in Christendom today. . . . [For] *only in this movement are all streams uniting, and all ministries being accepted and practised*" (pp. 149, 153).

Another characteristic of Neo-Pentecostalism is its theological diversity. Protestants and Catholics, conservatives and liberals do not automatically discard their own theological and ecclesiastical differences when they come together in this movement. Nor do the movement's leaders themselves agree on the precise definition of the Baptism of the Holy Spirit. Protestant Neo-Pentecostals, for instance, often view the Baptism of the Holy Spirit as a "second work of grace" after conversion, or as a special infilling of the Holy Spirit already living in the believer. Roman Catholics, on the other hand, look at the Baptism of the Holy Spirit as an interior experience (usually with outward manifestations) of the Spirit's filling and transforming power in the life of a believer who has received the Holy Spirit through the sacrament of water baptism. The exact nature of the *charismata* (such as tongues speaking and divine healing) and their operation as outlined in I Corinthians 12–14 is also debated. Nevertheless, it would be wrong not to suppose that Charismatic Renewal is indeed firmly rooted in historic Orthodoxy. Further, that implicit or explicit Orthodoxy is enhanced by the fact that whether one is theologically liberal or conservative, he will almost invariably come to have a vivid sense of God as a *person*, since in the Baptism of the Holy Spirit, God has *demonstrated* his reality to him in a personal way. Likewise, even if one's attraction to Scripture has been lost, the Pentecostal experience will restore interest in serious Bible study, and it will also give a new awareness of the efficacy of prayer. The Neo-Pentecostal, regardless of his theological outlook, must develop a fresh *openness* if he is to continue successfully within the movement.

Finally, we must emphasize the thoroughgoing reformist character of Charismatic Renewal. There is no interest in separating from the old ecclesiastical structures and building new ones according to the traditional denominational Pentecostal pattern. Rather, present institutions are to be renewed by the charismatic activity of the Holy Spirit as it affects the membership of a church through the continued presence *within* that structure of persons who have been baptized in or filled with the Spirit.

On the positive side, we have seen that Neo-Pentecostalism, as a valid expression of Orthodox Christianity, is serious about spiritual renewal by its Ecumenical and reformist stance. Perhaps its main strength lies in its spontaneity and in the fact it is still comparatively unstructured, knowing nothing of the "disease of institutional neurosis" that seems to be sapping the strength of the Church. But at the same time, there are three major dangers facing Charismatic Renewal at present. These are suggested by Michael Harper himself:

1. Anti-intellectualism and an unthinking fundamentalism is the first. . . . Pentecostalism in some people's minds is equated with a belief in the verbal inspiration of scripture (usually the King James version only), a kind of proof textualism, whereby chapter and verse answers every question, irrespective of the context. It seems to require a belief in the pre-millenial view of the Second Coming, and an almost complete distrust in theology. . . . The present-day charismatic movement, generally speaking, is not . . . a movement of unthinking fools floating on a wave of emotional experience. . . . But the danger is still there. An unthinking old-fashioned fundamentalism will always be a hindrance to the forward surge of the Holy Spirit.
2. The second danger is what many call today—pietism. . . . There comes all too easily a drawing away from the world in pursuit of more "spiritual" action, apart from the occasional sortie to capture some enemy prisoners. . . . When we are filled with the Holy Spirit there should be an immediate concern for the world in every area of its life. . . . Let [the movement] . . . lead Christians in a war against racism, the exploitation of the environment, inflation, property speculation and other evils of our age.
3. A third danger is elitism. This is a subtle form of human pride that divides Christians from one another. . . . The charismatic movement is in real danger the moment it thinks of itself as something apart from the rest of the Christian world.[14]

If Neo-Pentecostalism does, in fact, display tendencies toward Fundamentalism and literalism, social unconcern and spiritual elitism, the fact that at least one of its most highly respected leaders fully understands and is determined to correct these weaknesses is encouraging.

Like the New Evangelicalism and the Young Evangelicals, Charismatic Renewal gives strong evidence of a desire to maintain and renew the spirit of the New Testament and the primitive church in a secular age. Although it has not yet clearly manifested a positive social conscience, Neo-Pentecostalism displays a meaningful kind of unity in experience that Establishment Evangelicalism still argues is not possible apart from doctrinal agreement. Numerous New Evangelical thinkers and Young Evangelicals are attracted to that unity. Some even share the Charismatic experience and are involved in various institutions and organizations associated with the Neo-Pentecostalism—Oral Roberts University, Full Gospel Business Men's Fellowship International, the Kathryn Kuhlman ministry, Melodyland Christian Center in Anaheim, California, and the like. Perhaps Charismatic Renewal and the Young Evangelicals can continue to learn from each other, and even complement one another in their mutual quest for spiritual renewal and a whole Gospel relevant to every dimension of life. We shall consider this possibility and its implications for the Church universal later in our discussion.

III. A Thorn in the Side: Evangelicalism and the Contemporary Church

The mainline denominations will continue to exist on a diminishing scale for decades, perhaps for centuries, and will continue to supply some people with a dilute and undemanding form of meaning, which may be all they want. These dwindling denominations may spawn new movements which, if they pursue the hard road of strictness, may have vital effects on human life, such as the declining churches had in their youth but can no longer achieve.

Dean M. Kelley, *Why Conservative Churches are Growing*

If there is going to be a renascence of religion, its bearers will *not* be the people who have been falling all over each other to be "relevant to modern man." To the extent that modernity and secularization have been closely linked phenomena in Western history, any movement of countersecularization would imply a repudiation of "modern man" as hitherto conceived. . . . Ages of faith are not marked by "dialogue," but *proclamation.*

Peter Berger,
The Christian Century

Revival of church life always brings in its train a richer understanding of the Scriptures. Behind all the slogans and catchwords of ecclesiastical controversy, necessary though they are, there arises a more determined quest for him who is the sole object of it all, for Jesus Christ himself. What did Jesus mean to say to us? What is his will for us today?

Dietrich Bonhoeffer, *The Cost of Discipleship*

The real Ecumenical crisis of the present day is not between denominations *qua* denominations, or between Protestants and Roman Catholics. Nor is it, as Harvey Cox suggested in 1965, between traditional and experimental forms of church life. *The* Ecumenical pinch today is the increasingly apparent cleavage between Evangelicals, on the one side, and mainstream Ecumenical Liberals, on the other. While it might be possible to include the Fundamentalists in this problem as well, the fact of the matter is that Fundamentalism is neither ready nor willing to explore ways to resolve the issue through some kind of meaningful reconciliation between Liberalism and Orthodoxy. At any rate, the really important Ecumenical question of the 1970s has to do with *theology* rather than ecclesiastical institutions.

A. EVANGELICALS IN THE CHURCHES

In the course of our discussion so far, we have observed that since the Fundamentalist–Modernist controversy, Evangelicals have formed their own denominations and churches which are not related either to the National Council of Churches or the World Council of Churches. Instead, some of these have aligned themselves officially with the National Association of Evangelicals as an alternative. Also, membership of two major historic denominations, the Southern Baptist Convention and the Lutheran Church, Missouri Synod, is still, by and large, Evangelical. Finally, many Evangelicals have remained in the mainstream denominations affiliated with the NCC–WCC.

There are today in the United States close to 3 million Missouri Synod Lutherans and approximately 12 million Southern Baptists. Add to these at least 4 million Evangelicals within NAE denominations and other nonaligned churches. Then, we can estimate that out of the aggregate NCC constituency of over 42 million, perhaps 14 million or more consider themselves Evangelicals. That gives us a total of about 33 million churchgoing Evangelicals in America today. But this figure does not include those individuals presently alienated from the institutional church, such as the Jesus People; nor does it take into account the growing population of Pentecostals and other Evangelicals within the Roman Catholic Church. Also not included is the high percentage of

Evangelicals in the American Lutheran Church (2.5 million members), which is related to the WCC, but not to the NCC. And finally, various scholars have contended that the majority of Protestants in the United States who do not hold membership in any particular church tend to be theologically conservative, and thus basically sympathetic to the Evangelical position. The truth of this assertion is supported most vividly, of course, by the ever-increasing popularity of Billy Graham among the general public.

B. THE FALL AND THE RISE: LIBERALISM VS. EVANGELICALISM

Much has been made recently of the apparent decline of mainstream Ecumenical Liberalism and the simultaneous upsurge of Evangelicalism. We have already hinted at why this might, in fact, be the case. It now remains for us to take a look at the situation more closely.

The Liberal churches and historic denominations seem to be in trouble. Membership gains are not keeping step with the increase in population as a whole, and some denominations are actually losing members. Fewer young people are noticeable in local congregations, and budget cuts are clearly the order of the day. There is a tendency, moreover, for individual churches, unhappy with denominational and Ecumenical support of questionable causes, to redirect their funds from the respective national and international ecclesiastical organizations to *local* concerns. Consequently, these same denominations and Ecumenical structures have been forced to cut back their staff personnel dramatically and also withdraw financial aid from projects dependent on Ecumenical or denominational support, such as experimental and campus ministries.

Why exactly is mainstream Ecumenical Liberalism declining? Several reasons can be postulated. First, too many pastors and church executives are challenging the political and social values of their constituencies *without* adequate biblical-theological foundation for what they are saying and doing. Second, lacking solid biblical authority, these ministers are not providing satisfactory answers to the ultimate questions still asked by the average layperson. In other words, unsecular man wants to know who he is, why he is here, and where he is going. Third, members of Liberal churches are not being exhorted to a *meaningful* Christian commitment and discipline of faith. Fourth, by their neglect of traditional evangelism, Liberal pastors can hardly expect to attract new members in a time when the pervasive respectability once attached to church membership is declining. Today, most people feel no need to go to church unless they are receiving some kind of spiritual benefit as a result. But the historic churches and denominations seem to have failed in meeting the needs of their constituencies.

If Liberalism appears to be on the wane, there is growing evidence that Evangelicalism is experiencing a renaissance at the same time. Allowing for the tendency of conservative churches to inflate membership statistics, most Evangelical congregations appear to be holding their own at worst, and increasing their numbers dramatically at best. Given the Evangelical emphasis on tithing as a stewardship minimum, these same churches find little difficulty in meeting and expanding their annual budgets. To cite two extraordinary examples, the six thousand-member Melodyland Christian Center (independent Neo-Pentecostal) in Anaheim, California, operates on a budget in excess of 2 million dollars per year. And the First Baptist Church of Van Nuys, California, which is affiliated with the Conservative Baptist Association, has close to 10,000 members and an annual budget of 4 million dollars.

Outside the institutional church proper, Evangelical college and university campus groups for fellowship and evangelism are on the rise, while the mainstream United Ministries in Higher Education (UMHE), comprising many of the older denominational foundations, continues to cut staff and lose influence. In this connection, we have already mentioned the phenomenal success of Campus Crusade for Christ. But the more intellectually motivated Inter-Varsity Christian Fellowship (IVCF) is also doing well, as is the still burgeoning Jesus People movement in its various manifestations.

Charismatic Renewal and other comparatively unstructured Evangelical movements, such as Key 73, persist in attracting widespread support, even from some self-professed Liberals. The circulation of *Christianity Today* is at a record high, while its Ecumenical counterparts, *Christianity and Crisis* and *The Christian Century*, are fighting for their very existence. Evangelical publishing houses (such as Eerdmans, Zondervan, Word, Creation House, and Logos International) account for at least half of all religious books sold today. And secular publishers (such as Lippincott and Harper & Row) are producing Evangelical titles at an ever-increasing rate. While even the most prestigious Ecumenical divinity schools (such as Union, Yale, and Chicago) seem to be losing students, several prominent Evangelical seminaries (such as Fuller, Trinity, Gordon–Conwell, and Asbury) are showing significant gains in enrollment. Finally, we might also suggest that the recent nationwide popularity of old Gospel songs and hymns like "O Happy Day!" and "Amazing Grace" gives evidence of the continued relevance of the Evangelical message to contemporary man.

What then are the specific reasons why Evangelicalism appears to be on the rise in the wake of a declining Liberalism? Again, we could propose a number of possible causes. First, defectors from the Liberal churches can find answers to their ultimate questions and meaning for their lives in an Evangelical movement which holds firm to an authoritative Bible, demands a life-transforming conversion, and requires a strong personal commitment and spiritual discipline. And, as Dean Kelley, a United Methodist minister and NCC Director for Civil and Religious Liberty, says:

For when a handful of wholly committed human beings give themselves fully to a great cause or faith, they are virtually irresistible. They cut through the partial and fleeting commitments of the rest of society like a buzz saw through peanut brittle.

They are able to do this for several reasons: (1) They are willing to put in more time and effort for their cause than most people do for even their fondest personal ambitions. (2) They have an assurance, a conviction of rightness, of being on the side of God, that most people in most human endeavors cannot match. (3) They are linked together in a band of mutually supportive, like-minded, equally devoted fellow believers, who reinforce one another in times of weakness, persecution and doubt. (4) They are willing to subordinate their personal desires and ambitions to the shared goals of the group.[1]

This does not mean, of course, that *all* Evangelicals fit the aforementioned description. Clearly they do not. Nevertheless, Evangelicals come closer to a life-changing Christian commitment than do most mainstream Ecumenical Liberals.

Second, if the values of Middle America are indeed quite compatible with the beliefs and concerns of Establishment Evangelicalism, at least, it is only reasonable to suppose that the typical middle-class American searching for a dynamic religious faith could easily be adduced by an Evangelical theology that does not challenge his or her social and political values. In this respect, Billy Graham's cautious Evangelical reformism is far more appealing to the moderate stance of Middle America than either the activism of Harvey Cox's sometimes radical Liberalism or the reactionary conservatism of Carl McIntire's Separatist Fundamentalism.

Third, in view of the fact that we are living in an age of mounting anxiety and pessimism concerning the future of mankind, Dispensational apocalyptic—still the overriding interest of both Fundamentalism and a not insignificant segment of Establishment Evangelicalism—becomes particularly attractive to those religiously inclined Americans who discern *no* way out of a seemingly hopeless human situation apart from God's direct intervention in history to rapture his true Church *out* of this wicked and perverse world system.

Fourth, Evangelical Christianity offers *the* answer to the contemporary search for authenticity in living. Young people, especially, are revolting against the sterile routinization of modern existence. In ever increasing numbers, so it seems, they are following a risen Lord who claims to be "the Way, the Truth, and the Life," and the only source of a new birth and real life.

Fifth, there is a mounting acceptance within middle-class society of experiential and emotional religiosity. Evangelicalism, particularly in its Charismatic manifestation, emphasizes the *experience* of knowing God personally in Jesus Christ by the power of the Holy Spirit. And enthusiastic spirituality is often the result of this new inward quest for a dynamic, experiential faith to live by.

Sixth and finally, ours is an era in which the supernatural has been rediscovered. Modern man turns out to be far less secular than was hitherto supposed. Because Evangelical Christianity has always been open to the miraculous dimension of divine activity, we can understand why so-called modern man now tends to choose Orthodoxy over its overly demythologized counterpart.

It would perhaps be unfair to imply that the current upsurge of Evangelicalism *necessarily* means the ultimate death of the historic denominations per se. For although much Evangelical growth has indeed taken place outside the mainstream churches—and apart from the institutional church altogether—sentiment for the Evangelical position is also increasing *within* the grass roots constituencies of the historic denominations. We have mentioned, for instance, that the rapidly expanding Charismatic movement is plainly inclined to remain *inside* the mainstream churches as a force for renewal. It is also apparent that many other Evangelicals would prefer *not* to separate themselves from the wider fellowship of the Church universal as expressed in the historic denominations and the Ecumenical movement. But there is a major dilemma relevant to the matter in question. This problem, moreover, constitutes the single most important reason why the mainstream denominational and Ecumenical structures are, in fact, declining, and why even the most conciliatory Evangelicals find it difficult *not* to withdraw their support—if not themselves—from these ailing ecclesiastical institutions.

It goes without saying that, by and large, Protestants whose churches are not officially aligned with the NCC or WCC are alienated from the Ecumenical movement as a whole. But it is also the case that, despite their impressive numbers, Evangelicals *within* related denominations rarely hold positions of decision-making power either in the denominational or Ecumenical structures. Since mainstream Ecumenical Liberals control most NCC- and WCC-related denominational hierarchies, it is only logical that they should predominate in the Ecumenical organizations as well. After all, it is the aligned denominations themselves that make appointments to the more inclusive Ecumenical bodies.

For a long time, Liberals justified the striking absence of Evangelicals from Ecumenical leadership by arguing that Evangelicals refuse to listen to contrary points of view, and even if they *were* offered committee and executive positions, most leading Evangelical church men and women would decline! On the other hand, Evangelicals complain that it is because of their conservative theology that they have been systematically excluded from (1) both denominational and Ecumenical hierarchies, (2) faculty posts in leading seminaries, (3) teaching positions in college and university religion departments, (4) Ecumenical campus ministries, and (5) the editorial boards of Ecumenical journals and periodicals. Answering the charge of unwillingness to listen, Evangelicals admit that Liberals are indeed open to almost any contrary position—Catholic, humanist, even Marxist—yet, at the same time they utterly refuse to consider the Evangelical stance. As Carl Henry has said, today the only heresy is Orthodoxy.

There are signs, however, that mainstream Ecumenical Liberals and Evangelicals are finally beginning to move towards conciliation. Some WCC leaders are now urging more Ecumenical participation by Christians from unaffiliated churches and Evangelicals in general. It is also clear that one motive for restructing the NCC is to enlist support from nonaligned Pentecostals, Missouri Synod Lutherans, Southern Baptists and others of conservative theological persuasion.

But as yet there is little progress evident in the election and appointment of Evangelicals to positions of authority within the mainstream ecclesiastical structures. Cordial relations with Catholics of different kinds at Ecumenical gatherings somehow have an aura of respectability —even glamor. So, it is not surprising that increased Catholic participation at many levels of Protestant church life is openly encouraged. And, partly because of strong guilt feelings on the part of the majority, Blacks, women, young people, and other minorities are now readily accepted into Ecumenical leadership. But there has been less urgency to reconcile the Ecumenical–Evangelical cleavage. No guilt feelings are apparent.

At this point, we might suggest that the basic Ecumenical issue today is not *just* the existence side by side of two seemingly contrary schools of Christian thought—Orthodoxy and mainstream Ecumenical Liberalism. Nor is it merely that Liberalism appears to be dying, while Orthodoxy is enjoying a renaissance as the once-belittled opposition. The real Ecumenical problem goes deeper than that; it lies in the fact that mainstream Ecumenical Liberalism and Evangelicalism are becoming increasingly uncomfortable treading their separate paths, but neither school has yet found a workable method of effecting the reconciliation they both seem to desire. Dialogue, though always useful, has not been enough. And token Evangelical representation in denominational and Ecumenical hierarchies has also failed to bring about satisfactory results.

In a day when people are seeking a dynamic, if not experiential faith to live by, Evangelicals can play a significant role in whatever more fully united Church finally emerges. In this connection, one thing is certain. The political, social, cultural, and even theological concerns of a growing number of *younger* Evangelicals, at least, are drawing much closer to the priorities of mainstream Ecumenical Liberalism than is generally supposed. These Young Evangelicals and their older supporters have freed themselves completely from the old prejudices associated with the Fundamentalist–Modernist controversy and its aftermath, and are ready to move forward. We shall argue, therefore, that *they* offer the best hope for a meaningful Ecumenical–Evangelical reconciliation so desperately needed.

It now remains for us to take a close look at the young men and women whose positive beliefs and actions constitute what can only be termed a *revolution* in Orthodoxy. We shall then be able to discern just how this revolutionary biblical Christianity can lead to the transformation of both the Church universal and human society as a whole.

IV. Backgrounds To the New Discontent

Freud was perfectly right in asserting that all men oscillate between the death urge and the life urge. . . . What many churches have failed to realize is that in the teens and twenties the life urge very much predominates over the other. Christianity ought, accordingly, to be presented in terms of the challenge, the ideal, the adventure of making the very most out of life by putting the maximum into it. Instead, we find it presented in terms of the death urge, with the accent on duty, on conformity to accepted patterns of behaviour and speech, on sitting silent while the clergyman preaches and prays, on the comforts of the life to come, on the wisdom of sitting loose to the things of time and space! Is it any wonder that this makes little appeal to full-blooded young people?

Michael Green, *Runaway World*

In the past, they told us not to worry about changing society because what we need is to change men. New men will change society. But when the new men begin to worry about changing society, they are told not to worry, that the world has always been bad, that we await new heavens and a new earth and that this world is condemned to destruction. Why try to make it better? What's even worse is that those who teach this are the ones who enjoy all the advantages that this passing world offers, and they passionately defend them whenever they are endangered.

Samuel Escobar,
Is Revolution Change?

A loveless legalism is always the mark of a dying evangelicalism.

Reinhold Niebuhr, *The Atlantic Monthly*

55

Evangelicalism and Fundamentalism still converge in the basic demands
individual Orthodox churches place upon their members. A new convert
is expected immediately to adopt a life-style in accordance with the
specific dos and don'ts of the religious group he or she has joined.
Regardless of polity and theological differences, most nonsacramental
Evangelical and Fundamentalist congregations require faithful attendance at services, a program of regular Bible reading and private devo-
tions, and tithing as a minimum for stewardship. The convert must also
refrain from all forms of worldliness. Generally included here are prohi-
bitions against drinking, the use of tobacco, social dancing, gambling
and less often, card-playing, attendance at the theater, immodest dress,
and popular music (especially rock). These negative external demands
—reflecting revivalistic condemnation of evils associated with the wide-
open frontier towns—are cultural carry-overs (or "baggage") from the
nineteenth century. However, those churches not firmly rooted in
American revivalism are less likely to enforce these cultural taboos.

The fledgling believer tends to get prepackaged and usually pat answers to *all* his questions. In order to gain standing in his Fundamentalist or Evangelical congregation, a new convert is required to accept not
only a set pattern of behavior, but also certain mandatory (or fundamen-
tal) doctrines, *one* method of biblical interpretation, and very definitely,
an approved eschatology. Inherent in the value structure of most Orthodox churches, as Vernon Grounds, President of Conservative Baptist
Theological Seminary in Denver, suggests in *Revolution and the Christian Faith* (Phila. and N.Y.: Lippincott, 1971) lie (1) an overriding social
and political conservatism, (2) a distinct otherworldliness that nevertheless allows for material success, (3) a strong individualism and bourgeois
mentality, and (4) an unprophetic acquiescence to prevailing social
norms. As long as he submits without qualification to his church's
authority and conforms to its standards, the Evangelical or Fundamentalist can continue to enjoy its fellowship.

Young people, especially, are expected to capitulate to the authority
of their church. Orthodoxy has traditionally stressed to a high degree
Christian separation from the wider society; hence, the *most* socially
acceptable vocation its young people can choose is the ministry—"full-
time Christian service." Fundamentalist and Evangelical congregations
have always produced more than their fair share of pastors, missionaries,

youth workers, and the like. What is particularly unfortunate about this situation, however, is the fact that a young person who is not called into the ministry often feels like a second-class citizen in his own church. In their zeal to recruit full-time Christian servants, Orthodox congregations have lost an adequate understanding of what constitutes a Christian vocation (Romans 12 and I Corinthians 12). Very little effort is made to relate secular professions of any kind to the concept of Christian service. So, young people in Evangelical and Fundamentalist churches often believe that by *not* taking up a clearly ministerial vocation, they have somehow missed God's *perfect* will for their lives in favor of his always substandard *permissive* will. Some may harbor guilt feelings over this matter throughout the course of whatever career they finally select.

As we have said, Orthodox denominations and churches give ample encouragement to the aspirations of young people *they* think qualify for full-time Christian service. Suitability is judged by adherence to the *special* expectations a given church body sets out for its ministerial hopefuls. Typically, a young man makes his intent known by a public affirmation—often in response to an altar call through which he visibly dedicates his life to the service of God. Thereafter, he is expected to take an active part in the church youth program, to assume leadership over his peers, and to be ready with a personal testimony to his faith at any time. Likewise, his dress and external behavior must be above reproach.

Musical ability always enhances a young man's suitability for the ministry. If he does not play the guitar, piano, or another appropriate instrument, he can at least learn the basics of evangelistic song-leading (or "spiritual cheerleading," as it is sometimes called). As a song-leader, the ministerial hopeful becomes a natural M.C. at youth rallies, camps, and the more formal services of worship.

Quite often, the aspiring pastor will have participated in some kind of evangelism already in high school—maybe Youth for Christ or Young Life. (Founded in 1940–41, Young Life is a highly successful movement to reach for Christ completely unchurched youth of high school age. Its "life-style" evangelism is subtle and stresses meaningful interpersonal relationships without requiring adherence to any rigid theological system.) Upon graduation, his church will lead him in the direction of an acceptable college such as Wheaton or Westmont, if he can qualify for admission. While in college, the young hopeful will no doubt become actively involved again in student evangelism—working with organizations like Campus Crusade for Christ or, if his church does not get too suspicious, Inter-Varsity Christian Fellowship. During summer vacations, he may be offered employment at his home church—in the youth program.

When a ministerial candidate is ready for seminary, he must be very careful to choose the *right* school in conformity with what his pastor and the church board feel is best for him. For many churches, even the once-acceptable prominent Evangelical seminaries are now too liberal. Accordingly, schools holding a strict Dispensational stance such as Dallas Theological Seminary (and, to a lesser degree, Talbot Theological Seminary) are becoming increasingly attractive. As a graduate student in theology, the young hopeful may again be invited to spend his summers assisting with the youth program of his home church.

If all goes as planned, the seminary graduate will now be prepared to take on the duties typically associated with a level one assistant pastorate. He will be a youth minister as the first step in his career of full-time Christian service—molded in the stereotyped image of the Fundamentalist or Evangelical pastor and trained to reproduce in kind all over again.

Orthodoxy has not yet taken Women's Liberation seriously. In almost all non-Pentecostal Evangelical or Fundamentalist denominations, women are not ordained to the ministry. "Unmarriageable" types, however, may be encouraged by their churches to make the ultimate sacrifice —to become a missionary. Single females are welcome on the mission field, but not in the home pulpit. Alternatively, an aspiring young lady with a graduate degree in theology might be called by an Orthodox church to become an unordained director of Christian education—for less pay than her ordained male counterpart would get for the same job. But, for a marriageable young lady in the typical Fundamentalist or Evangelical congregation, the *highest* vocational aspiration she can have is to become the wife of a minister. Every Orthodox pastor—lest he be regarded as a playboy or, worse yet, a homosexual—must have a wife. In taking on a minister, the young woman will lose her identity completely. The ideal pastor's wife is simply an extension of her mate— sweet, sociable but not aggressive, talented, above reproach in her behavior and, above all, entirely submissive to the will and career of her husband. As such, she becomes a "nonperson" in every sense of the word.

A. YOUNG REBELS IN THE CHURCHES

The real crunch of all this comes, of course, when a member of an Evangelical or Fundamentalist church falls from grace by some measure of nonconformity to church standards or by even questioning those norms openly. An active layman will rarely be chided for his shady business dealings, his self-righteousness, or his superficial friendliness to persons outside his own circle of friends. (The church functions as the chief social outlet for the average Fundamentalist or Evangelical. Much of his free time is spent in a church where social stratification and cliques are manifestly apparent.) Behavior expectations in Orthodox Christianity do not ordinarily extend to deep-level interpersonal relations. But if a member of an Evangelical or Fundamentalist church breaks its cultural taboos, or goes through the tragedy of divorce, for instance, woe be unto him—especially if he holds a position of leadership within his congregation. The same proscription applies to the young person. (He usually does not have to worry about his standing in the church hierarchy, however, since even youth leaders and ministerial candidates are still often excluded from board membership in Fundamentalist and Evangelical congregations because of their "immaturity." Nevertheless, the wayward young man or woman will be spiritually and physically disfellowshipped from the "in group" so evident in most Orthodox churches.)

Especially sad is the case of the young ministerial hopeful who transgresses against his church. Just one flaw in his external conduct, one mistake in his sex life, one question raised to challenge his church's stance on *anything* may signal the end of that church's (and perhaps also his Christian parents') support of his pastoral aspirations. Quite frankly, Evangelical and Fundamentalist denominations and churches can be among the most *unforgiving* institutions anywhere.

The Young Evangelical, then, dissatisfied with the position espoused by his Orthodox church, and unhappy about the artificial role he must assume therein, is faced with a dilemma not easily resolved. On the one hand, he can always turn to Liberalism. But what does mainstream

Ecumenical Liberalism in its present state have to offer him? And, if he *remains* faithful to the authority of Scripture, the necessity of conversion, and the mandate for evangelism, he will probably be an unwelcome guest in most Liberal churches and a threat to their ideology. On the other hand, he can withdraw from the institutional church altogether. Yet, in so doing, he may lose the fellowship of like-minded believers he so desperately needs for his own spiritual development, and he will most certainly forfeit an important dimension of his commitment to the Church universal. It is not easy to be a Christian alone. The other option, of course, is for the Young Evangelical to remain in his own church—and fight!

Reacting against the values of Fundamentalism and Establishment Evangelicalism, some Young Evangelicals have been forced to leave the institutional church altogether. But an increasing number of them are now attempting to stay within their Evangelical (or even Liberal) denominations and churches, in the hope of *transforming* those structures into something better. It is a truism to say that young people as a whole are no longer content to be seen but not heard. The same applies to the Young Evangelicals. They *demand* a voice in their churches.

The new discontent among the younger representatives of Evangelical Christianity is becoming manifestly apparent. Motivated by the positive elements of student protest, the hypocrisy of the Orthodox churches, and the slow death of the Liberal denominations, the Young Evangelicals have been equipped to be the vanguard of a revolution in Orthodoxy under the leadership and in the power of the Liberator who promised to set men and women free from every kind of oppression. As Black Evangelist Tom Skinner challenged the delegates to the 1970 ICVF missionary convention in Urbana, Illinois, "You will never be radical until you become part of that new order [God's kingdom] and then go into a world that is enslaved, a world that is filled with hunger and poverty and racism and all those things of the work of the devil. Proclaim liberation to the captives, preach sight to the blind, set at liberty them that are bruised, go into the world and tell men that are bound mentally, spiritually and physically, *'The liberator has come!'* "[1]

B. INTELLECTUAL ROOTS

This emerging revolutionary movement, moreover, is not without a strong biblical–theological foundation. It has intellectual roots which can be traced directly to the thought of C. S. Lewis and Dietrich Bonhoeffer, the deepest concerns of biblical Orthodoxy, and most of all, the founding and subsequent development of Fuller Theological Seminary.

1. C. S. Lewis

A tutor for many years at Oxford University's Magdalen College, and later professor of Medieval and Renaissance literature at Cambridge until his death in 1963, C. S. Lewis proved once and for all that Orthodox Christianity *is* intellectually defensible. (Ironically perhaps, as James Houston noted in an article in the April 1972 *Right On*, Lewis was sufficiently ahead of his time that while a teacher at Oxford he was rarely invited to speak to Evangelical groups and he had little or no contact with their leaders.) In the words of Elton Trueblood:

One of the best things C. S. Lewis did, in his truly remarkable career, was to make readers critical of the absurd, though widely accepted, notion that the enemies of the gospel have a monopoly upon intellectual acumen. If he did nothing else, he turned the tables! The old Devil of the *Screwtape Letters* warned his nephew against letting people *think*. "The trouble about argument," he said, "is that it moves the whole struggle onto the Enemy's own ground."[2]

Walter Hooper of Jesus College, Oxford, Lewis's one-time personal secretary, describes him as the most thoroughly *converted* man he had ever met: "Christianity was never for him a separate department of life; not what he did with his solitude; 'not even,' as he says in one essay, 'what God does with His solitude.' His whole vision of life was such that the natural and supernatural seemed inseparably combined."[3]

It was very hard for the most able unbeliever to deal effectively with C. S. Lewis's formidable logic and great learning. As a layman—and a good match for many theologians—his apologetics for Christian Orthodoxy are profound, yet easily understood. Lewis viewed the Christian faith as utterly reasonable; and blessed with a keen wit, he demonstrated the rare ability to poke fun at his critics *and* himself without forsaking the seriousness of the questions being raised. Above all, Lewis was always concerned about the contemporary relevance of the Gospel—an interest which was evident in his work long before the concept became fashionable. In his famous apologetic, *Mere Christianity* (New York: Macmillan Paperbacks, 1960), the pipe-smoking, claret-drinking academician successfully did away with all the ecclesiastical and cultural trappings usually associated with Orthodoxy *without* undue demythologizing in the process. He says on page 6: "ever since I became a Christian I have thought that the best, perhaps the only, service I could do for my unbelieving neighbours was to explain and defend the belief that has been common to nearly all Christians at all times. . . . Our divisions should never be discussed except in the presence of those who have already come to believe that there is one God and that Jesus Christ is His only Son." And again, on pages 130 and 131:

I think all Christians would agree with me if I said that though Christianity seems at first to be all about morality, all about duties and rules and guilt and virtue, yet it leads you on, out of all that, into something beyond. One has a glimpse of a country where they do not talk of those things, except perhaps as a joke. Everyone there is filled full with what we should call goodness as a mirror is filled with light. But they do not call it goodness. They do not call it anything. They are too busy looking at the source from which it comes.

Those who are well aware of Lewis's strong defense of the miraculous in human life might be surprised to learn that he was also a friend of modern science (though he by no means worshiped the theory of evolution or any other scientific proposition) and, as a literary critic himself, accepted the *positive* results of biblical criticism—from a position of faith in Christ and submission to the authoritative character of Scripture's teaching. This stance can be illustrated by the following passage:

The Old Testament contains fabulous elements. The New Testament consists mostly of teaching, not of narrative at all: but where it *is* narrative, it is, in my opinion, historical. As to the fabulous element in the Old Testament, I very much doubt if you would be wise to chuck it out. What you get is something *coming gradually into focus*. First you get, scattered through the heathen religions all over the world—but still quite vague and mythical—the idea of a god who is killed and broken and then comes to life again. No one knows where he is supposed to have lived and died; he's not historical. Then you get the Old Testament. Religious ideas get a bit more focused. Everything is now concerned with a particular nation. And it comes still more into focus as it goes on. Jonah and the Whale, Noah and his Ark, are fabulous; but the Court history of King David [II Samuel 2—I Kings 2] is probably as reliable as the Court history of Louis XIV. Then, in the New Testament the *thing really happens*. The dying god really appears—as a historical Person, living in a definite place and time. If we *could* sort out all the fabulous elements in the earlier stages and separate them from the historical ones, I think we might lose an essential part of the whole process. This is my own idea *(God in the Dock,* pp. 57–58).

By this kind of positive critical approach to the Bible, the Oxbridge don, as a layman, foreshadows the basic attitudes now expressed by theologians of the New Evangelicalism.

Contrary to an assumption widely held in Orthodoxy, C. S. Lewis rejected unequivocally the notion that *all* men and women at any given moment can be counted either among the saved or the lost. For him, the human condition suggests something far more complex and therefore less subject to the judgmental whims of self-righteous Christians:

The world does not consist of 100 per cent Christians and 100 percent non-Christians. There are people (a great many of them) who are slowly ceasing to be Christians but who still call themselves by that name: some of them are clergymen. There are other people who are slowly becoming Christians though they do not yet call themselves so. There are people who do not accept the full Christian doctrine about Christ but who are so strongly attracted by Him that they are His in a much deeper sense than they themselves understand *(Mere Christianity,* p. 176).

Yet, Lewis also affirms the Christian mandate for evangelism. His whole life as an apologist for Orthodox Christianity testifies to that concern. And while he stresses the fact that there are indeed *numerous* methods for bringing individuals into the kingdom of God—"even some ways that I specially dislike!"—Lewis at the same time is quick to chide those who in their dialogue are so anxious to accommodate unbelievers that they lose the *distinctives* by which the world can recognize them as followers of Christ: "As Christians we are tempted to make unnecessary concessions to those outside the Faith. We give in too much. Now, I don't mean that we should run the risk of making a nuisance of ourselves by witnessing at improper times, but there comes a time when we must show that we disagree. We must show our Christian colours, if we are to be true to Jesus Christ. We cannot remain silent or concede everything away" *(God in the Dock,* p. 262). (This tendency, of course, is the bane of mainstream Ecumenical Liberalism.)

Finally, we can say that C. S. Lewis conveys to his readers a sense of discipleship. Here was a man who enjoyed life immensely—one who must have delighted in the conviviality of High Table at Oxford and Cambridge. (In Cambridge and Oxford colleges, students dine at "Low Table," while faculty and their guests eat at "High Table" [i.e., raised from the floor], which tends to be more formal—and elegant—and at which better food and drink are generally served.) Yet he was a profoundly committed Christian as well. In a very real sense, Lewis was *in* the world but not *of* the world. He was a thoroughly *converted* man, so much so that others readily discerned that quality in him. Perhaps the secret of being in the world but not of it lies in an individual's willingness to let go, to give up his life completely for the sake of Christ—only to get it back again infinitely more alive than before. The person whose anchor is in heaven has all the freedom he needs to be fully human in the world, because he *knows* that Jesus is Lord and that his kingdom ultimately will prevail. Thus C. S. Lewis concludes his argument in *Mere Christianity:*

Give up yourself, and you will find your real self. Lose your life and you will save it. Submit to death, death of your ambitions and favourite wishes every day and death of your whole body in the end: submit with every fibre of your being, and you will find eternal life. Keep back nothing. Nothing that you have not given away will ever really be yours. Nothing in you that has not died will ever be raised from the dead. Look for yourself, and you will find in the long run only hatred, loneliness, despair, rage, ruin, and decay. But look for Christ and you will find Him, and with Him everything else thrown in (p. 190).

To summarize, then, we can enumerate several good reasons why the Young Evangelicals have been so greatly influenced by this master of Christian apologetic. First, Lewis demonstrated clearly by his own life that an Orthodox believer in Jesus Christ can *think* and in so doing can offer a rational defense for his faith. In other words, your mind matters.

Second, he was not only capable of self-criticism but could laugh at himself in the process. Orthodoxy, we must admit, has not been known for its good sense of humor. Third, Lewis's brand of Orthodox Christianity is so utterly *reasonable* that neither science, biblical criticism, nor the learned skeptic, on the one hand, nor obscurantism on the other, could weaken it. Fourth, this thinker, when questioned about his Christian convictions, was able to say yes and no in truth *without* alienating his unbelieving neighbors. He was both a scholar *and* a gentleman. Fifth, Lewis proved that an Orthodox believer can *enjoy* life—that he is just as human as he is spiritual. And finally, he manifested by his life and work that conversion to Christ runs deeper than a moment's decision or mere assent to a list of doctrines. Conversion, for C.S. Lewis, is a spiritual transformation; and conversion in action is discipleship.

2. Dietrich Bonhoeffer

Born in Breslau, Germany, in 1906, Dietrich Bonhoeffer was the son of a university professor and leading authority on psychiatry. His ancestors included theologians, professors, lawyers, and artists. From his mother's side, aristocratic blood flowed in his veins. Bonhoeffer was raised in Berlin, in the Christian, humanitarian, and liberal tradition of his parents, and early came to love nature, music, art, and literature. He was a gracious, congenial person, full of charm and noble character. People were attracted to this unselfish and self-sacrificing man, and he made friends easily wherever he went. Educated at the Universities of Tübingen and Berlin, Bonhoeffer became lecturer in systematic theology at Berlin University when he was only twenty-four years of age. A splendid career as theologian and Lutheran pastor seemed to lie ahead of him, but the young academician took Christian discipleship seriously.

Bonhoeffer had been trained in the school of theological Liberalism but was profoundly influenced by the Neo-Orthodoxy of Karl Barth. Yet, after his chosen vocation was well under way, something dramatic happened to this man that would change the course of his life:

I hurled myself into my work in an unchristian and unhumble manner. . . . Then something else came along, something which has permanently changed my life and its direction. . . . I had often preached, I had seen a lot of the church, I had talked and written about it, but I had not yet become a Christian. (I know that until then I had been using the cause of Jesus Christ to my own advantage.)

The Bible, most particularly the Sermon on the Mount, has freed me from all this. Since then everything has changed. . . . I now realize that the life of a servant of Jesus Christ must belong to the church, and step by step it became clearer to me to what extent this must be so.[4]

We might say, then, that Dietrich Bonhoeffer had been converted in the deepest sense of that word. His role in the German resistance and Confessing Church, his arrest by the Nazis in 1943 and subsequent execution in 1945, are all well known. G. Leibholz says of Bonhoeffer in his memoir introducing Bonhoeffer's inspiring *The Cost of Discipleship* (2nd edition, New York: Macmillan Paperbacks, 1963):

What Dietrich Bonhoeffer and others did cannot be expected from the many. The future in modern society depends much more on the quiet heroism of the very few who are inspired by God. These few will greatly enjoy the divine inspiration and will be prepared to stand for the dignity of man and true freedom and to keep the law of God, even if it means martyrdom or death (p. 33).

Thus Bonhoeffer's life and death have given us great hope for the future. He has set a model for a new type of true leadership inspired by the gospel, daily ready for martyrdom and death and imbued by a new spirit of Christian humanism and a creative sense of civic duty. The victory which he has won was a victory for us all, a conquest never to be undone, of love, light and liberty (p. 35).

The young German theologian was a man who spent many hours in the study of Scripture, in prayer and devotion. He placed high value on Christian fellowship and "the communion of saints." One of Bonhoeffer's fellow prisoners was an English officer, Payne Best, who tells of the martyr's last sermon:

Sunday 8th April, 1945, Pastor Bonhoeffer held a little service and spoke to us in a manner which reached the hearts of all, finding just the right words to express the spirit of our imprisonment and the thoughts and resolutions which it brought. He had hardly finished his last prayer when the door opened and two evil-looking men in civilian clothes came in and said: "Prisoner Bonhoeffer, get ready to come with us." Those words "come with us"—for all prisoners had come to mean one thing only—the scaffold.

We bade him good-bye—he drew me aside—"This is the end," he said. "For me the beginning of life," and then he gave a message to give, if I could, to the Bishop of Chichester. . . . Next day, at Flossenbürg, he was hanged.[5]

Thus Dietrich Bonhoeffer lived out the reality of his own words: "When Christ calls a man, he bids him come and die" (p. 99). At the same time, he was convinced that, for him, death would be merely "the beginning of life."

The work and example of Bonhoeffer has attracted the admiration of conservative and liberal alike. But it is his profound understanding of *discipleship* that has been especially meaningful for the Young Evangelicals. Reacting against sacramental efficacy on the one hand, and "works righteousness" on the other, modern Orthodoxy emphasizes *grace* as the key to salvation. That we are saved by grace through faith alone has always been the central message of Orthodox Christianity in general and revivalism in particular. Unfortunately, this grace has too often been linked with *one* moment of time in the life of a believer—that moment in which he *first* confesses his sin and accepts Jesus as his Savior. In Orthodoxy, "first-step salvation," as we shall term it, tends to end where it begins. Jesus becomes personal Savior, so it seems, but his *lordship* thereafter is not really taken seriously. Justification, then, predominates over sanctification, or the life of discipleship. Bonhoeffer calls grace without discipleship "cheap grace":

Grace is represented as the Church's inexhaustible treasury, from which she showers blessings with generous hands, without asking questions or fixing limits. Grace without price; grace without cost! The essence of grace, we suppose, is that the account has been paid in advance; and, because it has been paid, everything can be had for nothing. . . .

Cheap grace means the justification of sin without the justification of the sinner. Grace alone does everything, they say, and so everything can remain as it was before (pp. 45–46).

Cheap grace is grace without discipleship, grace without the cross, grace without Jesus Christ, living and incarnate (p. 47).

For Bonhoeffer, cheap grace is "the deadly enemy of our Church" (p. 45). But "costly grace" is something entirely different:

Costly grace is the gospel which must be *sought* again and again, the gift which must be *asked* for, the door at which a man must *knock.*

Such grace is *costly* because it calls us to follow, and it is *grace* because it calls us to follow *Jesus Christ.* It is costly because it costs a man his life, and it is grace because it gives a man the only true life (p. 47). . . .

We must . . . attempt to recover a true understanding of the mutual relation between grace and discipleship. The issue can no longer be evaded. It is becoming clearer every day that the most urgent problem besetting our Church is this: How can we live the Christian life in the modern world? . . .Happy are they who, knowing that grace, can live in the world without being of it, who, by following Jesus Christ, are so assured of their heavenly citizenship that they are truly free to live their lives in this world. Happy are they who know that discipleship simply means the life which springs from grace, and that grace simply means discipleship (p. 60).

In *The Cost of Discipleship*, Dietrich Bonhoeffer repudiates the shallow conception of God's grace as "showers of blessings" without cost. He affirms that just as faith without works is dead, so grace without discipleship is of no effect. More important, however, this young pastor-theologian manifested by his own life—by his costly resistance to an inhuman political tyranny—that the true believer must not only take up his cross, he must also be willing to be crucified on it. Conversion to Jesus Christ does indeed have a beginning, but the really converted life must be renewed continually; hence, Luther declares that as Christians we are converted *daily.* If C. S. Lewis introduced the joy of discipleship to the Young Evangelicals, Bonhoeffer demonstrated to them its cost.

3. Words Into Deeds: Translating Orthodoxy's Deepest Concerns Into Action

As expressed by the most articulate leaders of the contemporary Evangelical movement already in its beginnings, three major concerns emerged which would become pivotal interests in biblical, classical or historic Orthodoxy (as opposed to the cultic Orthodoxy of Fundamentalism). We have described those concerns as a firm commitment to (1) the inspiration and authority of Scripture in matters of faith and practice, (2) the necessity of personal conversion to Jesus Christ, and (3) the mandate for evangelism. In addition to these, we might also add as important (4) the search for Christian unity without the loss of theological distinctiveness, (5) an outreach to the secular world without accommodation to its system, (6) the quest for absolutes in ethics without legalism, (7) genuine social concern, and (8) an intellectually motivated faith grounded in the deeply experiential knowledge of God as a person through Christ.

The Young Evangelicals share the same concerns of biblical Orthodoxy but are distressed by the fact that these interests have largely *failed* to take root and grow within the ecclesiastical institutions of Establishment Evangelicalism. Commitment to the Bible's inspiration and authority has led almost to the worship of the biblical text. Conversion to Christ has not meant discipleship, while the mandate for evangelism has capitalized more on numbers and the "spiritual" dimension of the Gospel than on meeting the needs of the whole person. The search for spiritual unity, of course, has still not gotten off the ground, and separation from the world has predominated over a loving outreach to a physically, mentally, and spiritually oppressed humanity. The quest for absolutes in ethics has produced yet another legalism which elevates external behavior connected with the cultural baggage of revivalism and offers no forgiveness to those who fail to meet its expectations. Social concern has been characterized either by extreme caution or by reaction, while the *authority* of personal religious experience together with a lingering anti-intellectualism have hindered the *further* development of a rational apologetic for the Gospel in the midst of a secular society.

We can say, then, that the deepest concerns of historic Orthodoxy, and the thought and living example of utterly committed Christians like C. S. Lewis and Dietrich Bonhoeffer, have pricked the conscience of the Young Evangelicals with respect to the failures of their own theological tradition. At the same time, it has been the function of *one* Evangelical seminary, in particular, to demonstrate by its teaching and its very existence that Evangelicals themselves, especially the young, *can* work effectively to eradicate the weaknesses in their tradition and in the process build a truly revolutionary biblical Orthodoxy.

4. Fuller Theological Seminary

H. Richard Niebuhr suggests that the theological school is the "intellectual center of the Church's life."[6] If this is so, it is only natural that the newly emerging Evangelical movement of the 1940s should be motivated to found a seminary representative of its own concerns both to exhibit academic excellence *and* to apply biblical faith to the mounting complexities of modern life. In the minds of Evangelical leaders, neither the Fundamentalist schools nor the seminaries dominated by Liberalism were taking *both* concerns seriously.

In May 1947, Charles E. Fuller of the "Old Fashioned Revival Hour" radio broadcast and Harold John Ockenga, then pastor of the Park Street Church, Boston, met together with four Evangelical scholars in downtown Chicago to launch Fuller Theological Seminary. Located in Pasadena, California, Fuller enrolled thirty-nine students in the first entering class in the fall of 1947. Charter faculty members included Ockenga as president, Carl Henry, and Harold Lindsell. Original funds for the seminary came from the estate of Henry Fuller, Charles Fuller's father and the school's namesake.

In the fall of 1953, Fuller Seminary moved out of the buildings of the Lake Avenue Congregational Church onto its own campus. By then, the student body had risen to 250, and there was a faculty of fifteen, most of whom held doctorates from leading universities in the United States and abroad. During Edward John Carnell's five-year presidency from 1954, Fuller won full accreditation by the American Association of Theological Schools (1957) and added several key faculty and board members. Carnell resigned the president's position in 1959 to devote himself once again to full-time teaching and research, while Ockenga resumed the presidency until 1963, when the board elected David Allan Hubbard to the post.

Hubbard, an ordained Conservative Baptist minister, is a graduate of Westmont College, Fuller Seminary, and St. Andrews University in Scotland, which awarded him the Ph.D. in Old Testament. At the time of his election as Fuller's third president, Hubbard was teaching at Westmont—where his presence must have made numerous conservative board and faculty members increasingly uncomfortable. Under this young president's guidance, the seminary initiated its own Th.D. program and founded two satellite schools—World Mission and Psychology —both of which were accredited by the Western Association of Schools and Colleges in 1969. Fuller's School of Psychology awards the Ph.D. degree.

Present enrollment (1972) includes approximately 460 graduate students from nearly every state and several foreign countries. These seminarians represent forty-five denominations and come from almost

200 colleges and universities. Fuller's enrollment is increasing on the average of 10 percent a year, and over 1,220 men and women have taken advanced degrees and serve as pastors, assistant pastors, teachers, chaplains, counselors, youth leaders, and denominational executives throughout the world.

Faculty members subscribe to a biblically Orthodox statement of faith which includes as an important part of its mission the Church's corporate responsibility to strive for social justice and relieve human distress and need. The seminary's annual budget amounts to nearly one and one-half million dollars, of which close to 50 percent comes from gifts, bequests, grants and, endowment funds. Board members include noted Evangelical businessmen, ministers, educators, as well as Billy Graham, and Black Evangelist William Pannell of Tom Skinner Associates.

Fuller Seminary's curriculum leading to the first professional degree in theology—Master of Divinity (M. Div.)—is well rounded. In addition to Greek and Hebrew (now dropped as a requirement by many Liberal schools), and the more traditional theological disciplines, the program also stresses contemporary concerns reflected by courses in fields like social ethics, race relations, and psychology, as well as by practical education for urban ministry. Fuller's only rule of conduct is *maturity;* "sensitivity training" is mandatory for all students. And chapel services, though not required, are nonetheless well attended.

By their stature, teaching, publications, and their loyalty to the institutional church and the Church universal, the faculty of Fuller Theological Seminary has provided a model to its students and graduates, and through them to the Young Evangelicals in general, of what modern biblical Orthodoxy can be—of its explicit revolutionary potential. Unlike the Fundamentalist schools, Fuller is not polemically anti-intellectual. And in contrast with the mainstream Ecumenical seminaries and their Liberal denominational counterparts, it still regards theology as *serious* business, involving questions of ultimate significance. Social concern is most certainly important at Fuller, but not to the exclusion of its fostering personal Bible reading and a meaningful devotional life. The faculty of Fuller Seminary tend to inspire their students in the Christian faith rather than encourage their doubts. Unlike Fundamentalist institutions, differences of opinion among faculty at this school are tolerated and discussed *openly.* There is a strong attempt to let students and faculty alike *think* for themselves. By giving seminarians a chance to hear representatives of contrary schools of thought who are regularly invited to the campus, Fuller offers its students the opportunity to determine what stance is right *for them*. And all this is done within a community of faith which is mutually supportive of the needs of both faculty and students.

In the wake of Fuller's success, other Evangelical seminaries have pursued its example. In this category, we might include Asbury, Gordon-Conwell, Conservative Baptist Theological Seminary in Denver, and Bethel Theological Seminary (Baptist General Conference) in St. Paul, Minnesota. Even Trinity Evangelical Divinity School (Evangelical Free Church of America) in Deerfield, Illinois, founded in part as a reaction to Fuller's "too liberal" approach, seems to be following suit as well. But Fuller Theological Seminary was the first school of its kind, and clearly still the best.

Having traced the chief intellectual roots of the present discontent among the Young Evangelicals, we shall now consider their theological, social, political, and cultural concerns specifically in order to determine both the nature of revolutionary Orthodoxy and, then, its ultimate importance for the life of the Church universal.

V. Revolution in Orthodoxy

I hate, I despise your feasts,
and I take no delight in your
solemn assemblies. . . .

Take away from me the noise of your songs;
to the melody of your harps I will not listen.
But let justice roll down like waters, and righteousness
like an ever-flowing stream.

Amos 5:21, 23, 24

Woe to you, scribes and Pharisees, hypocrites! for you cleanse the outside of the cup and of the plate, but inside they are full of extortion and rapacity. You blind Pharisee! first cleanse the inside of the cup and of the plate, that the outside also may be clean.

Woe to you, scribes and Pharisees, hypocrites! for you are like whitewashed tombs, which outwardly appear beautiful, but within they are full of dead men's bones and all uncleanness. So you also outwardly appear righteous to men, but within you are full of hypocrisy and iniquity.

Matthew 23:25–28

Despite the constant repetition of this formula by many—not all —evangelicals, it has yet to be shown that the converted individual "inevitably" becomes the challenger of structured social evils. What about the multitudes of "saved" slaveholders in ante bellum USA who, far from rising up against what John Wesley called that "execrable sum of all villainies," American slavery, defended it? It was when, under common grace, saved and unsaved became

cobelligerents in the struggle to end the system that a crucial
social victory was won.

Paul S. Rees of
World Vision International

The priorities of the Young Evangelicals can be separated roughly into
four major areas of concern. First, there is an interest in developing a
richer understanding of the inspiration and authority of Scripture as the
basis for action in the world. Second, it is felt that evangelism must
always be the proclamation of the Gospel in its *entirety*—relevant to the
whole man or woman and *all* his or her needs. Third, there is a new
emphasis on discipleship and on discovering values appropriate to the
transformed life in Christ. And finally, it is believed that the insitutional
church should function corporately not only as the community of the
saved but also as an instrument of reconciliation—calling alienated men
and women to be reconciled to God, to one another, and to their own
true selves.

A. THE BIBLE AS ABSOLUTE

The Young Evangelicals accept Scripture as *both* history and revelation. They view the redemptive historical events recorded therein as the
mighty acts of God, culminating in the life, death, and resurrection of
Jesus Christ. But for them, the Bible also embodies the divinely given
Word of God as spoken by the prophets, and which interprets Christ's
earthly mission and his future coming to establish the eternal kingdom
of God. So, it is the conviction of the Young Evangelicals that Scripture
is both revelation and history, word *and* deed.

1. George Ladd and Positive Biblical Criticism

One of the most important biblical scholars of the New Evangelicalism is George Ladd, professor of New Testament at Fuller Theological
Seminary. Ladd's book, *The New Testament and Criticism* (Grand Rapids: Eerdmans, 1967), moreover, has been particularly influential regard-

ing the thought of the Young Evangelicals. In it, he examines the use
and abuse of the various types of biblical criticism—textual, linguistic,
literary, form, historical, and comparative religion—with the conviction
that "an evangelical understanding of the Bible as the Word of God
written is not *per se* hostile to a sober criticism; rather, an evangelical
faith demands a critical methodology in the reconstruction of the historical side of the process of revelation" (p. 215).

Ladd does not try to *answer* all the questions raised by criticism. He
stresses the fact that an Evangelical criticism "must often be satisfied
with hypotheses, probabilities, possibilities, rather than in dogmatic
certainties, as distasteful as this may be to the uncritical mind which
insists on 'thus saith the Lord' in every detail of Bible study" (p. 216).
The Fuller professor suggests, in addition, that the most significant
characteristic of Scripture is its dual nature—at the same time the Word
of God *and* the words of men recorded in a specific historical time and
context. But he is quick to point out that the Bible does not merely
contain the Word in some sense, nor is it just a vehicle of or witness
to the Word of God. God acted in redeeming history (i.e., that kind of
history not explained by a secular historiography), yes; but he also spoke
through the prophets as they spoke and wrote: "The result is not a mere
product of history or religious insight; it is a normative, authoritative,
divinely initiated and superintended account of who God has revealed
Himself to be and what He has done for man's salvation" (p. 216).

Nevertheless, if Scripture is indeed "the inspired Word of God, the
Christian's only infallible rule for faith and practice" (pp. 216–217), this
does not mean that infallibility extends to all historical details. It clearly
cannot include the preservation of an infallible text, nor an infallible
lexicography, nor infallible answers to all questions about authorship,
sources, and dates, nor even an infallible reconstruction of the historical
situation in which revelation occurred and in which the books of the
Bible were written. God has left these matters to human scholarship,
and that, of course, is always *very* fallible.

Finally, George Ladd maintains that a proper biblical criticism does
not wish to criticize the Word of God per se, but rather, it makes a
concerted effort to understand *how* that Word has been given to man.
Such criticism is positive, because it does not proceed on the negative
assumption that certain supernatural or supra-historical events recorded
in Scripture could *not* have occurred. Rather, it lets God be God, and

seeks constructively to facilitate a better comprehension of the spiritual message of salvation by uncovering as best as possible the historical setting in which that message was first made known to believing men and women. Thus, the Fuller Seminary professor concludes his book:

Here is perhaps the greatest miracle of the Bible: that in the contingencies and relativities of history God has given to men His saving self-revelation in Jesus of Nazareth, recorded and interpreted in the New Testament; and that in the New Testament itself, which is the words of men written within specific historical situations, and therefore subject to the theories and hypotheses of historical and critical investigation, we have the saving, edifying, sure Word of God. In hearing and obeying the Word of God, the scholar must take the same stance as the layman: a humble response which falls to its knees with the prayer, Speak, Lord, for thy servant heareth (p. 218).

Committed to the same spirit of Ladd's positive and constructive biblical criticism, the International Fellowship of Evangelical Students, rejecting "wooden literalism" and the classical theory of verbal inspiration with its implicit notion of divine dictation, is now also moving in a direction where the complete reliability of Scripture is found to have a "wider and richer meaning than infallibility and inerrancy" as traditionally understood. For this international organization of Young Evangelicals:

Scripture is entirely trustworthy in the sense that its message conveys the true knowledge of God and His works, especially the way of salvation. . . . Proper interpretation takes into account the sacred writers' intentions, use of language, style and contexts. It also consistently acknowledges the divine origin of Scripture and its organic unity. It not only requires the use of philological and historical sciences, but also unqualified submission to the teaching of Scripture and prayerful dependence upon God's Holy Spirit.[1]

2. Repudiation of Dispensationalism

Few mainstream Ecumenical Liberals are aware of the degree to which Dispensationalism has permeated Orthodox Christianity throughout the world as a result of the widespread popularity of the *Scofield Reference Bible* (and its newly revised successor, *The New Scofield Reference Bible*), prophetic conferences, the Bible institutes and colleges, revivalism and—more recently—the best-selling books of

Hal Lindsey. If Liberals are generally ignorant of the nature of Dispensational theology, most Fundamentalist pastors and laypersons and many Evangelicals as well have been led to believe that Dispensationalism provides the *only* method of biblical interpretation and the *only* eschatology that can legitimately be called Orthodox. But nothing could be farther from the truth.

One of the most informative critiques of Dispensationalism as a highly complex theological system has been written by Clarence Bass, professor of theology at Bethel Seminary, St. Paul, Minnesota. In his book, *Backgrounds to Dispensationalism,* (Grand Rapids: Eerdmans, 1960), Bass traces the origins of this basically pessimistic ideology directly to J. N. Darby, founder of the Plymouth Brethren. Born the son of a well-to-do Irish family in London, England, in 1800, Darby was educated at Westminster School, London, and Trinity College, Dublin, where his scholarly bent became apparent. During the course of his life, Darby would produce a significant theological literature which, collected together, comprises thirty-two volumes.

The continuity of Dispensational thought from Darby to the present time can be delineated in an unbroken succession of theologians from his contemporaries to the faculty of Dallas Theological Seminary today. Although there are various subtle differences of interpretation expounded by the theoreticians of Dispensationalism, certain distinguishing features of the system always seem to be manifested in one way or another. Bass discusses all of them; but it is our purpose to mention here only those which are particularly offensive to the Young Evangelicals.

First, there is a rigid and artificial periodization of history that *emphasizes* mankind's continuing failure to please God:

> Scofield defines a dispensation as "a period of time during which man is tested in respect of obedience to some specific revelation of the will of God." He adds further: "these periods are marked off in Scripture by some *change* in God's method of dealing with mankind, in respect to two questions: of sin, and of man's responsibility. Each of the dispensations may be regarded as a new test of the natural man, and each ends in judgment—marking his utter failure in every dispensation" (p. 19).

In other words, God places humanity under different responsibilities and conditions his action toward man according to each failure. But with respect to this periodization of history, the Bethel theologian suggests,

"Of such divisions and differentiated relations the historic Christian faith knows nothing. No such doctrine can be found in standard texts in any age of the history of the church" (p. 21).

Second, Dispensationalism requires a *literal* interpretation of Scripture, especially the prophetic sections, to the exclusion of all other methods of biblical exposition. In this connection, Bass says of those who hold the Dispensational view: "They insist on an unconditional literal fulfillment of all prophetic promises, failing to realize that by its very nature prophetic utterances are sometimes allegorical or symbolic" (p. 22). At the same time, there is no appreciation of the *ethical* dimension of prophecy or of its *conditional* fulfillment. Contrary to this understanding of prophecy, however, Vernon Grounds maintains that biblical prophecies concerning the future must be seen as contingent upon human action. Citing the examples of King Hezekiah and the city of Nineveh (II Kings 18–20), he argues that sincere repentance on the part of individuals and nations in response to prophetic warnings can forestall or even cancel predicted events. Says Grounds, "The fulfillment of prophecy is neither automatic nor unconditional."[2]

Third, the Dispensational position demands belief in a separate and secret coming of Christ to remove (i.e., "rapture") the Church for a seven-year period *prior to* his coming in power and glory. This short span of seven years on earth without the Church is termed the Great Tribulation during which time Antichrist reigns and just before which human society is marked by increasing depravity, while the mainstream church structures are characterized by rampant apostasy. The idea of Christ's rapturing the Church *out* of the world prior to his millennial rule is based primarily upon—so most Dispensationalist laypersons believe—I Thessalonians 4:16, 17: "For the Lord himself will descend from heaven with a cry of command, with the archangel's call, and with the sound of the trumpet of God. And the dead in Christ will rise first; then we who are alive, who are left, shall be caught up together with them in the clouds to meet the Lord in the air; and so shall we always be with the Lord." But notice the strained exegesis demanded. Even if this passage is taken literally, it says nothing about a rapture in the Dispensational sense. And it certainly does not declare that the Church will be taken out of the world only to return at a later time. To arrive at such a conclusion, clearly, one must fit these verses into the general Dispensational scheme. In fact, John F. Walvoord himself admits that the notion of a pre-tribulation rapture is based more upon a specific theological understanding of the nature of the Church than on anything else: "It is . . . not too much to say that the rapture question is determined more by ecclesiology than eschatology. . . . Any answer to the rapture question must therefore be based upon a careful study of the doctrine of the Church as it is revealed in the New Testament" (quoted in Bass, p. 39).

In Dispensational theology, then, getting ready for the rapture becomes the all-embracing concern of the Church. If we are indeed living in the Last Days—just before the great "catching up"—social, political and ecclesiastical *progress* is necessarily excluded.

Fourth, Dispensationalism demands, implicitly at least, a *compartmentalization* of Scripture. No single passage in the Bible can have primary application to two dispensations at the same time. Certain parts of the biblical text, moreover, may be restricted to certain people, while entire groups may be exempt from others. As Clarence Bass suggests: "If, as dispensationalism avows, the church was not instituted until Pentecost, none of the Gospels apply directly to the Christian: the sermon on the mount, the Lord's Prayer, the ethical teaching of Jesus —these are all "kingdom [i.e. millennial] truths." . . . [Even] the Book of Acts must then be divided between those passages referring to the Jew and kingdom and those referring to Gentile and church" (p. 38). We can easily understand, therefore, why the social exhortation of the Old Testament prophets and the ethical teaching of Jesus are so rarely stressed, or even discussed, in Fundamentalist and Evangelical pulpits. It is *Paul*, rather, who is accepted by Dispensationalists as *the* exponent of theological and ethical truth for the "dispensation of grace"—the present age of the Church. Commenting on this point, Bass goes on to say: "Since the canonization of the New Testament, a unitary view of the Bible has been the guiding principle of interpretation for the church. A continuity in the message of the Scriptures has been accepted as the basis for understanding it. Dispensational compartmentalization is a departure from the historic faith" (p. 38).

Fifth and last, there is an underlying if not explicit theme in Dispensationalism concerning the *apostate* nature of Christendom. Ecclesiastical organization has "corrupted" the visible, institutional church. Taking this theme to its logical conclusion, the Church universal, then, can in no wise be described in terms of a recognizable, structured entity, but *only* in terms of the spiritual relationship of the believer to Jesus Christ. In this connection, Bass remarks:

The church is heavenly, not earthly: the individual believer is not baptized into a church here on earth, but into a heavenly relation with Christ.

In practical consequences, this caused Darby to distrust all organized ecclesiastical systems (though he created one himself). Two ideas, the individual *heavenly* relation to Christ as constituting the church, and the distrust of ecclesiastical systems, combined to establish a spirit of separatism in Darby's movement. All who did not agree with Darby's interpretation were characterized as "Not having the truth" or as "not understanding the divine plan of the ages," and therefore as somewhat "apostate" (pp. 46–47).

Such, of course, is the separatist stance that Dispensationalism in its various manifestations still tends to take today.

To summarize the distinguishing features of Dispensational thought which are especially offensive to the Young Evangelicals, we can enumerate the following: (1) a rigid and artificial periodization of history, emphasizing mankind's continuing inability either to do good or to please God; (2) an insistence on the literal interpretation of the Bible apart from any other method, together with a stress on the predictive sense of prophecy and its unconditional fulfillment; (3) an all-embracing concern to get ready for the rapture while enjoying all the material benefits this passing world has to offer; (4) a convenient compartmentalization of Scripture that avoids ethical demands; and (5) a belief in the apostate nature of Christendom which rejoices in the divisions—institutional and spiritual—separating the Body of Christ. (Incidentally, it is interesting to note the tendency among many Dispensationalists to identify as the Antichrist-Beast [Revelation 13, 17] prominent national or world political leaders who take the side of the oppressed and downtrodden or who work avidly for peace.)

Dispensationalism, then, is basically a method of biblical interpretation and an eschatology which diverges in numerous ways from the stance of historic Orthodoxy. Pessimistic in outlook, socially unconcerned, and separatist by nature, it is a nineteenth-century aberration, even from historic premillennialism (which allows for Christ's Second Coming prior to his millenial reign on earth—but does not accept a secret rapture of the Church, seven-year Great Tribulation, an exclusively literal interpretation of prophecy, or a compartmentalization of Scripture. Nor does historical premillennialism hold to an unduly pessimistic evaluation of the human situation during the Last Days so as to impede reform and progress in the sociopolitical and ecclesiastical arenas). Hence, is it any wonder that the Young Evangelicals have repudiated the Dispensational position so thoroughly?

B. EVANGELISM: REACHING THE WHOLE PERSON

If mainstream Ecumenical Liberalism has accepted in principle the premise of secular Christianity that evangelism *is* social action—without the call to repentance and personal commitment to Christ as Savior and Lord—Orthodoxy has traditionally maintained either that evangelism is the proclamation of the necessity of repentance and faith in Christ (as a purely spiritual act) alone, or that the new birth is the first step to an inevitable social concern. New persons, declares Establishment Evangelicalism, will build a new society. The problem, however, is that exponents of Orthodox evangelism have neglected the fact that human life has both a personal *and* a social component. Furthermore, they have somehow failed to realize that new persons have *not* inevitably produced a new society. Thus, in the minds of the Young Evangelicals, evangelism must reach the *whole* person—his spiritual needs, yes; but also his life in corporate society, his relationship with other men and women and the social structures they create for themselves. This conviction that conversion, discipleship and social concern are inextricably linked together is well articulated by Emilio Castro:

Conversion means that we become aware of a relationship with Jesus Christ, and this means, in time, relationship with our neighbor. It means becoming part of the discipleship of those who serve. These two elements—relation with Jesus Christ and relation with my neighbor—can be distinguished, but they cannot be separated. . . . The lack of a correct relationship with one's neighbor is authentic proof of the absence of the correct relation with God. Conversion understood as a personal advantage does not exist. It is always understood as a call to form part of the movement of God's ministry of love to the world.[3]

When the average American considers evangelism, he probably thinks of Billy Graham—and for good reason. Graham, perhaps, has brought more individuals to an *initial* saving encounter with God in Christ than any other person in history. For this reason alone, he surely deserves praise. Furthermore, to his credit, Billy Graham has been no friend either to denominational separation or to Protestant–Roman Catholic division. He has, therefore, enjoyed the support of Roman Catholics and Protestants alike. In addition, the mass evangelist has evidenced *some* forthright social concern. In the early days of the civil rights struggle, Graham spoke out boldly against racial segregation and integrated his own crusade staff. During the presidency of Lyndon Johnson, he gave his blessing to the War on Poverty. Without hesitation, Graham urged Richard Nixon in 1968 to select antiwar U.S. Senator Mark Hatfield (R–Ore) as his running mate. And recently, the mass evangelist was a featured speaker at the South African Congress on Mission and Evangelism held in Durban. There he made known his opposition to the South African government's policy of apartheid, and spoke to the largest multiracial audience (45,000) ever assembled in that country. (For twenty-five years prior to this engagement, Graham had refused invitations to preach in South Africa because of previous government insistence that strict racial segregation be observed at all his meetings.)

Yet, Billy Graham has proved to be a mounting disappointment to the Young Evangelicals. For despite his spoken and written support of prophetic social action and costly discipleship in principle, Graham's actual stance on concrete issues—apart from those just mentioned—has been noticeably weak. For one thing, the mass evangelist still declares that spiritually transformed men will *inevitably* produce a transformed society but fails to account for the fact that saved individuals are often (probably most often) supporters of the status quo rather than social change. And we may recall how when confronted with his failure to condemn the President's renewed bombing of Hanoi in December 1972, Graham responded by saying that God had called him to be a "New Testament evangelist"—not an "Old Testament prophet." Such may indeed be the case; nevertheless, the Young Evangelicals cannot understand how *any* committed Christian privileged to counsel the highest leaders of government can rightly refrain from standing up for social righteousness when sin becomes so manifestly apparent. Thus, because of Graham's increasingly unprophetic link with the powers that be, he was not invited to address Inter-Varsity's triennial missionary convention either in 1970 or in 1973—an honor he once regularly enjoyed.

In this connection, the Young Evangelicals have not only discerned Billy Graham's seemingly hypocritical stance on important social issues and his unabashed identification with the political establishment, they have also seen in him a foremost exponent of what Robert Bellah calls the "American civil religion." (The concept of "civil religion" comes from Rousseau's *The Social Contract.*) According to Bellah, this religion, comprising a set of religious beliefs, symbols and rituals emanating from the American historical experience interpreted in the dimension of transcendence,[4] supports the American Way of Life and gives credence to the notion of America's special destiny as guardian of liberty. The God of America's civil religion, moreover, is "much more related to order, law, and right than to salvation and love."[5] As Will Herberg suggests:

This American culture-religion is the religious aspect of Americanism, conceived either as the common ground of the three "faiths" [Protestantism, Catholicism, and Judaism] or as a kind of super-religion embracing them. . . . Americanism thus has its religious creed, evoking the appropriate religious emotions; it may, in fact, be taken as the civic [or civil] religion of the American people.

But civic religion has always meant the sanctification of the society and culture of which it is the reflection, and this is why Jewish-Christian faith has always regarded such religion as incurably idolatrous. Civic religion is a religion which validates culture and society, without in any sense bringing them under judgement. . . . Religion becomes, in effect, the cult of culture and society, in which the "right" social order and the received cultural values are divinized by being identified with the divine purpose. . . .

In a more directly political sense, this religiosity very easily comes to serve as a spiritual reinforcement of national self-righteousness and a spiritual authentication of national self-will. Americans possess a passionate awareness of their power and the justice of the cause in which it is employed. The temptation is therefore particularly strong to identify the American cause with the cause of God, and to convert our immense and undeniable moral superiority over Communist tyranny into pretensions to unqualified wisdom and virtue. . . . Aside

from occasional pronouncements by a few theologians or theologically minded
clergymen, religion in America seems to possess little capacity for rising above
the relativities and ambiguities of the national consciousness and bringing to
bear the judgment of God upon the nation and its ways.

. . . In its crudest form, the identification of religion with national purpose
generates a kind of national messianism which sees it as the vocation of America
to bring the American Way of Life, compounded almost equally of democracy
and free enterprise, to every corner of the globe; in more mitigated versions, it sees
God as the champion of America, endorsing American purposes, and sustaining
American might.[6]

Hence, civil religion merges together the cross and the flag, Christian
faith and patriotism.

A Young Evangelical, Joe Roos of the People's Christian Coalition in
Deerfield, Illinois, illustrates by way of criticism in the Spring 1972 issue
of *The Post-American* how Billy Graham's concerns and those of the
American civil religion are clearly compatible:

Graham not only fails to condemn American corporate sin with the same
vigor that he condemns personal sin, but he frequently identifies with that
American system which creates so much evil in the world. This is seen most
explicitly in his "Honor America" speech at the Lincoln Memorial, Washington
D.C., July 4, 1970. Seven reasons for honoring America were given.

First, we honor America because she has opened her heart and her door
to the distressed and the persecuted of the world. . . . For two centuries
America has been a land where the persecuted, the alienated, and the
refugees have come to find new opportunities and new freedoms.

(Witness the "opportunities" and "freedoms" of the oppressed and exploited
minorities of Indians, Blacks, Chicanos and Puerto Ricans.)

Second, we honor America because she has been the most generous nation
in history. We have shared our wealth and our faith with a world in need.

(Witness the gratitude of military dictators and generals throughout the world
who have received American military and economic aid in exchange for cooperation with American military and economic goals.)

Third, we honor America because she has never hidden her problems or
faults.

(Witness Daniel Ellsberg and the Pentagon Papers.)

Fourth, we honor America because she is honestly recognizing and courageously trying to solve her social problems.

(Sixty percent of the federal budget goes to defense.)

Fifth, we honor America because she has never sought to use her tremendous power to take over other nations.

(Ask the peoples of the world who have felt the brunt of American oppression and exploitation—Indochina, Brazil, Guatemala, Cuba, Chile, Dominican Republic, *ad infinitum, ad nauseam.*)

Sixth, we honor America because she defends the right of her citizens to dissent.

(Witness the right to dissent of the students shot at Kent State and Jackson State and beaten in Chicago, Columbia, Berkeley, etc.)

Seventh, we honor America because there is woven in the warp and woof of our nation faith in God.

It is here that Graham fails to distinguish between the God of American civil religion and the God of Judeo-Christianity (pp. 9–10).

If the values suggested by the mass evangelist seem indeed noble (though unfulfilled), they are rooted more deeply in the Declaration of Independence, the Revolution, and the Civil War than in Scripture. Thus, the American civil religion reflected in these values is still in marked contrast with the prophetic essence of historic Christianity, as Roos goes on to explain:

Our God is the God of Abraham, Moses, Peter and Paul—not Jefferson, Washington, Johnson and Nixon. Our values are predicated upon the transcendent norms of a loving Father who has revealed Himself in Jesus Christ—not an austere Provider of Blessings who gives a religious dimension to the developing American experience. A commitment to our God demands prophetic judgement upon a corrupt and sinful society and a lifestyle consistent with His transcendent norms—not passive submission to the State every time it uses religious language, motifs, and symbols to justify American expansionism (p. 10).

For the Young Evangelicals, then, Billy Graham's preaching of first-step salvation alone neglects the call to discipleship. Since it is a message of spiritual regeneration which also reinforces the often "sub-Christian" concerns and values of the WASP majority, that proclamation is necessarily the embodiment of cheap grace which justifies sin more than the sinner. At best, it is only half the Gospel. The Young Evangelicals seek in evangelism the call to faith *and* works, conversion *and* discipleship. They wish to support and undertake themselves an evangelism that will speak with the force and conviction of a Billy Graham and require the life dedication of a Dietrich Bonhoeffer as well—an evangelism that proclaims costly grace and demands the cross. In the words of the German martyr:

Once again, Jesus calls those who follow him to share his passion. How can we convince the world by our preaching of the passion when we shrink from that passion in our own lives? On the cross Jesus fulfilled the law he himself established and thus graciously keeps his disciples in the fellowship of his suffering. The cross is the only power in the world which proves that suffering love can avenge and vanquish evil. But it was just this participation in the cross which the disciples were granted when Jesus called them to him. They are called blessed because of their visible participation in his cross (*The Cost of Discipleship,* p. 161).

1. The New Mass Evangelism: Leighton Ford

At this point, we should remind ourselves that the present criticism of Billy Graham by the younger generation of Evangelicals is a recent phenomenon. There was a time when the mass evangelist's social stance —especially on racial justice and love—was far ahead of his Evangelical constituency. Indeed, it has only been within the last few years—as his ties to the political establishment grew stronger and he became Middle America's most admired personality—that Graham's reversal of his earlier public commitment to social concern manifested itself.

Mainstream Ecumenical Liberals have always been unhappy with Billy Graham. But what most people do not realize is the fact that those same Liberals must share at least some of the blame for the mass evangelist's retreat from a once-prophetic social position. For when he *did* in the past take a firm stand on racial justice and costly social involvement in general, mainstream Ecumenical Liberals most often either held their silence or continued to chide him for not doing enough. They should have understood that their vocal support of *every* prophetic action Graham took—however little it might have seemed to them— could have served as positive reinforcement for that action. In taking a social position unpopular among Evangelicals, the mass evangelist, of course, lost the support of his own people. But, despite his frequent Ecumenical gestures, Graham at the same time gained no significant praise or reassurance from the Liberal side to counterbalance Evangelical criticism. And it is no secret that any man or woman is strengthened by encouragement—from whatever quarter—when that person champions a controversial and unpopular cause. So where were the mainstream Ecumenical Liberals *then?*

Now, however, a more important question might be—is there yet hope for Billy Graham? In a rare expression of kindness coming out of Liberal circles, John Coleman Bennett, as a preface to his criticism of Graham's eschatology, recently remarked of the mass evangelist: "Billy Graham has a strong personal appeal as a man of integrity and grace, with a remarkable openness of spirit. He is fair to his critics, ecumenical in outlook, and willing to cooperate more than his theology would seem to permit. In the early days of the civil rights movement he took important symbolic action in refusing to speak to segregated audiences, and in other ways began to give a good personal witness on issues of racial justice."[7] If Bennett's evaluation is correct, then Graham—unlike say Billy James Hargis or Carl McIntire—*could* be persuaded to change his present stance in the same way he modified his outlook early in his ministry. Thus, the Young Evangelicals might be unwise to write off Billy Graham completely at this time. In fact, they probably should continue to support his evangelistic work when called upon to do so, but with a forthright criticism of his policies from within when they are clearly wrong. For criticism from Graham's own constituency—biblically based and constructively irenic—is more likely to be effective than what appears to him as unfounded destructive criticism lodged from the outside. Evangelicals are still committed to a miracle-working God—one who is certainly able to convince Billy Graham that a New Testament evangelist in this day and age can be an Old Testament prophet as well.

It should also be made clear at this point that by constructively criticizing Graham's social and political conservatism which detracts from the liberating power inherent in the Gospel he has been called to proclaim, the Young Evangelicals are not at the same time repudiating mass evangelism in general. For instance, the evangelistic altar call in public—no less than believer's baptism at a crowded beach—can be viewed as a chance for the new convert to make a meaningful symbolic affirmation of his faith in the midst of a secular society. And, *within* the ministry of mass evangelism, a most encouraging development has recently taken place—the emergence of a promising young evangelist out of the Billy Graham Evangelistic Association itself, Graham's own brother-in-law, Leighton Ford. A Canadian by birth, Ford is an ordained evangelist in the Presbyterian Church in the United States (Southern) and specializes in reaching college and university students for Christ. In this connection, the young evangelist was a featured speaker at Inter-Varsity's Urbana '70 missionary convention as Billy Graham's replacement.

From the beginning, Ford has taken a positive stance on the integral relationship between evangelism and social concern. A good example of his characteristic approach is Ford's three-week crusade in Seattle, Washington, where already in 1967, his concerns were apparent. The main speakers there, apart from himself, were four Washingtonians whose conversion to Jesus Christ had led them into prophetic social action. One had been motivated to start Job Therapy—an employment program for exconvicts. A second told how he had been led to sponsor a young prisoner who needed help desperately. The third speaker described how she had been motivated to work in a neighborhood house tutorial program aimed at low-income families; while the last discussed his decision to become a missionary surgeon in Korea.

During that crusade, 1,500 out of 75,000 who attended meetings responded to Ford's customary appeal for commitment to Christ. But another kind of appeal was made on Christian Action night. At that time, the young evangelist distributed a form listing ten fields of service that required volunteers immediately. People were asked to respond to the call. In addition, a special offering was taken for rehabilitation of prisoners and for two War on Poverty efforts. Thus Ford had broken with the stereotyped revivalistic tradition concerned only about meeting "spiritual" needs.

Leighton Ford espouses what he terms *revolutionary evangelism*— a ministry that effectively links traditional evangelism with positive social concern. Says the young evangelist in his book *One Way to Change the World* (New York: Harper & Row, 1970), "Again, compassionate social action should not be confused with evangelism; neither should it be separated from it. Like love and marriage, they go together" (p. 114). Developing his point further, Ford links biblical faith with the revolutionary stance: "Have we stopped to think that when we as Christians preach the Gospel we are in a sense sowing the seeds of revolution? The rights of men to freedom, dignity, and respect come directly from the Bible, from the story that God made man and God loves man and that the Son of God laid down His life for man. This is the ultimate source of human worth" (p. 10).

Commenting on the current racial crisis in America, the young evangelist speaks prophetically to the Evangelical churches: "Well, let me ask what kind of Gospel we are preaching when a church sends missionaries to convert Africans but suggests to the black man at home that he go to his own church with his own kind? Why should the Negro listen to us talk about a home in Heaven when we refuse to make him at home in our neighborhood and our school?" (p. 59). In this regard, Ford offers some concrete suggestions to Evangelicals who are serious about correcting racial injustice and hatred, and who honestly want to "build bridges" between the various races:

And further, we can let God show each of us a place where we can build a bridge. . . . This will mean sharing the Christ who can change men's hearts. It will mean supporting laws that oppose all kinds of discrimination. Laws can't make people love one another but they can help to prevent flagrant injustice. We can make friends with those of other races. Church leaders can arrange programs of exchange visits with people from churches of other races and make sure that their own churches are known to be open to all races in Christ's name. Businessmen and union officials can help open up places for individuals from minority groups [i.e., "affirmative action"] (pp. 65–66).

It is almost a truism to say that one of the weakest aspects of traditional evangelism has been its implicit and explicit self-righteousness and its bad manners. Speaking at Urbana '70, the young evangelist firmly rejected such behavior:

We do not evangelize from a superiority complex. We do not go in an attitude of condemning others. We must not say, "You're all wet and I've got all the answers." As D. T. Niles said, "We're beggars telling other beggars where to find bread." We go saying, "Brother, we're in the same boat. I identify with you. We've both failed. But Jesus Christ has enabled me to take my mask off and to face myself and admit my failures and prejudices. He's given me the way out, the exit. And this Jesus Christ can do the same for you. I'm not what I should be. I'm not what I'm going to be. But because of him, I'm not what I used to be!"[8]

Finally, Leighton Ford unreservedly repudiates the "Second Coming cop-out" so often associated with contemporary mass evangelism—the belief that since Jesus is coming soon, "we'd better get ready for the rapture" while the world goes to hell in the process. Says the young evangelist:

The hope of Christ's return is no escapist clause. It is not an out for Christian complacency, nor an alibi for noninvolvement. On the contrary, it is a spur to holiness, to evangelism, to obedience. It is a motivation to make God's work on earth our own, for Jesus told us in parable form to "occupy until I come" (Luke 19:13). Like Martin Luther we are to live and work as though Jesus Christ died yesterday, rose today, and is coming again tomorrow (*One Way*, p. 118).

In demonstrating by word and deed that evangelism and compassionate social action "go together like love and marriage," Leighton Ford has taken one step—one *crucial* step—beyond Billy Graham's (at best) second-priority social concern. And by putting Christ's Second Coming —the Blessed Hope of the Church—in its proper perspective as a *motivating* force for social transformation rather than a convenient excuse for inaction or reaction, he gives evidence of embracing the whole Gospel—one that can meet the needs of men and women as individuals *and* the very real needs of society as well. Thus Ford's revolutionary evangelism might well prove to be an important dimension of the present revolution in Orthodoxy taking place among the Young Evangelicals.

2. Campus Evangelism: Inter-Varsity Christian Fellowship (IVCF)

Inter-Varsity Christian Fellowship (IVCF) as a campus ministry of evangelism is the American outgrowth of the Evangelical student movement in England which took organizational form in 1928 when the various Evangelical Christian Unions (i.e., campus Bible-study and fellowship groups) at British universities banded together in the Inter-

Varsity Fellowship (IVF) of Evangelical Unions. (Already in 1909, the Cambridge Inter-Collegiate Christian Union had disaffiliated itself with the increasingly liberal Student Christian Movement.) IVCF is also the largest regional constituent of the International Fellowship of Evangelical Students (IFES), based in Lausanne, Switzerland. Organized in 1947, the IFES is the Evangelical counterpart to the rapidly declining mainstream Ecumenical Liberal World Student Christian Federation in Geneva.

IVCF operates from headquarters in Madison, Wisconsin, while InterVarsity Press (in cooperation with its British affiliate) publishes a good number of books by Evangelical authors aimed at the college and university communities, and issues a highly sophisticated, award-winning monthly—*HIS* magazine from Downers Grove, Illinois.

Founded in 1940, IVCF has grown rapidly, and chapters are active on many university and college campuses throughout the United States. IVCF is intellectually motivated and engages in a low-key "fellowship evangelism" carried on within small groups of students that meet regularly. Minimally paid regional staff members advise campus chapters and help organize new groups as well. Often confused with Campus Crusade for Christ, IVCF operates on a different principle altogether. Campus Crusade is just that—a direct approach *crusade* which stresses personal confrontation, "pressed-for" decisions and large numbers of converts; while IVCF is a *fellowship* of believers supporting one another in Christian growth. Both are evangelistic. But IVCF rejects Crusade's often anti-intellectual direct approach in favor of a more subtle discipleship-oriented evangelism through Bible-study and fellowship groups. And unlike Crusade, IVCF encourages questioning and a positive critical study of Scripture.

Until recently, IVCF was associated either with social noninvolvement or the same cautious social concern characteristic of Establishment Evangelicalism. In this sense, it reflected the traditional upper-middle-class orientation of the British IVF. The Oxford and Cambridge Inter-Collegiate Christian Unions (OICCU and CICCU respectively) have especially been entrenched in the British Public School tradition and the Evangelical wing of the established Church of England. At one time, the life of a committed CICCU or OICCU member was devoted almost exclusively to three pursuits—study, sport, and the Christian

Union. And within the Christian Unions themselves, political and social action were not considered as legitimate concerns for spiritually minded students.

The social stance of IVF has changed, however, particularly in the Christian Unions of the newer provincial universities where more students came from working-class backgrounds. Social concern and involvement have indeed become an important part of Christian witness for an increasing number of IVF members in Great Britain according to Andrew Walls, Head of the Department of Religious Studies at the University of Aberdeen, Scotland. But during the last few years, IVCF in the United States has far surpassed its British counterpart with respect to a deep understanding of the social dimension of the Gospel. This new priority was evidenced by the speakers and the attitudes expressed at Urbana '70. Every three years, IVCF sponsors an international missionary convention at the University of Illinois at Urbana. The triennial congress serves as a recruiting-ground for students interested in overseas Christian service. In earlier years, delegates to the Urbana conventions listened to staid professors, prominent athletes and famous preachers like Billy Graham talk about the "spiritual" dimension of life alone. But not in 1970.

Featured speakers for Urbana '70 included militant Black Evangelist Tom Skinner, Leighton Ford, antiwar Mennonite Myron Augsburger, social critic Samuel Escobar of IVCF in Canada, and master exegete John Stott. Reflecting the contemporary world cry for liberation, the convention's collected addresses were entitled *Christ the Liberator*. Speakers addressed themselves to topics such as student power, social concern, racial tensions, and revolution as they bear upon the mandate for evangelism. About 12,300 college and university students, many of whom displayed counterculture dress and manners, were in attendance at Urbana '70, where traditional hymnody had been replaced by Gospel-rock and Black soul music.

The Young Evangelicals attending Urbana '70 gave their most enthusiastic response to Tom Skinner, a former Harlem gang leader. They stood and cheered his blistering attacks on the hypocrisy of middle-class white America and the complacency of Evangelical churches which still contribute to institutionalized racism and poverty. They wholeheartedly supported his biting criticism of Wall Street, big business, "surburban bliss" and the "myth of democracy." Skinner then urged his Inter-Varsity listeners to become personally involved in the struggle to free men and women throughout the world from *every* kind of oppression —physical, mental, and spiritual—by going in the power of Jesus Christ, the Liberator. For anyone who is willing to join that new revolution, declares the Black evangelist in *Christ the Liberator,* God is ready "to saturate the common clay of man's humanity and then to send that man in open display into a hostile world as a living testimony that it is possible for the invisible God to make himself visible in a man" (p. 197).

If what happened at Urbana '70 was something of an astonishment to Establishment Evangelical and mainstream Ecumenical Liberal alike, more surprises are very likely in store in the future. At this point, we should perhaps mention the fact that the roots of IVCF's fresh under-standing of the integral relationship between evangelism and social action, faith and discipleship, can be traced not only to the student movement of the 1960s, but also to the writings of scholars connected with IVCF in Great Britain. Influential authors in this category, whose prime concern has been to relate biblical faith to the demands and complexities of modern life, include John Stott, rector of All Souls Church, Langham Place, London, and honorary chaplain to the Queen; Canon Michael Green, principal of St. John's College, Nottingham; and J. N. D. Anderson, professor of Oriental laws at the University of London, first chairman of the House of Laity of the General Synod of the Church of England, and Anglican delegate to the World Council of Churches. Furthermore, by encouraging its members to study, ques-tion and *think,* IVCF itself has sown the seeds of the new social aware-ness now emerging within its ranks.

Finally, we must not neglect the fact that featured speakers at Urbana '70 challenged the Young Evangelicals in attendance to become *person-ally* involved in a practical demonstration of love for one's neighbor. John Alexander, IVCF President, urged the delegates to translate their social concern into positive *action:*

But how can we, as we go from here, take the initial steps in loving our neighbor? Here are two tangible suggestions. First, when you are back home, ask the Lord to guide you to one person who is suffering. He may be suffering emotionally, physically or economically. And then go and do something to help him because you love him and because Jesus told you to do it. . . .

The second suggestion is this: Ask the Lord to show you one problem, one social ill, one injustice that needs to be corrected. And then work on it.[9]

Not uncommonly, a climate of social activism breeds a new kind of hypocrisy. By thinking only of the *collective* good of large groups—classes, races, nations, or the masses, a man may salve his conscience without personal involvement in the suffering of *individuals.* While he *talks* social concern, his own life-style—neighborhood, home, furniture, car, dress, food, drink, recreation, friends, church—may underscore the fact that he is still living "high off the system" he says he bitterly opposes. A supposed *social* conscience, then, becomes in reality an excuse for *personal* complacency. But Christian discipleship—grounded in costly grace—demands self-sacrificing, costly action. We are living in a day in America when real social witness to the gospel is likely to bring far more persecution than will traditional evangelism without social action. In this connection, Alexander's concrete proposals at Urbana '70 are modest; nevertheless, if Inter-Varsity as a whole (and other Evangelicals as well) take his concluding remarks seriously, the present revolution in Orthodoxy will surely be strengthened that much more.

3. Campus and Street Evangelism: Christian World Liberation Front (CWLF)

The Jesus People have produced numerous movements and groups displaying varied religious styles and ideologies. Some of these, despite their adoption of counterculture dress and manners, still hold to the basic values of their parent churches and Middle America in general. Others stress the "spiritual" side of the Gospel alone, emphasize personal religious experience, and are so keenly expectant of the imminent Second Coming that nothing else really matters. But still others, firmly rejecting the hypocrisy of American society and its ecclesiastical institutions, *are* trying to integrate into a whole the personal and social dimensions of the Gospel by espousing a truly radical yet biblical expression of Christianity. One such organization is a ministry of campus and street evangelism in Berkeley, California—Christian World Liberation Front (CWLF). Like IVCF, CWLF is as much concerned about Christian growth and discipleship as it is about evangelism per se.

In the wake of the mounting intensity of the student rights movement during the late 1960s, a small group of adults then working with Campus Crusade for Christ in Berkeley decided in 1969 to found a viable, socially concerned street and campus ministry as an alternative to the secular reform and revolutionary movements thriving in that city at the time. To counterbalance the secular Third World Liberation Front, then gaining momentum on the University of California campus, these forward-looking adult Evangelicals named their new organization the Christian World Liberation Front—a *family* of Christians working and ministering under Jesus Christ, the Liberator. One of the group's founders was Jack Sparks, a former professor of statistics at Pennsylvania State University, who is now chief facilitator of the movement.

From the beginning, CWLF modeled its program after the concerns and basic life-style of the counterculture. The organizers felt that this was the only way to reach students and street people in typically radical Berkeley. Two of the brothers in "God's forever family" have even written a counterculture paraphrase of selections from the New Testament epistles—*Letters to Street Christians.*

First of all, CWLF sponsors Bible raps, marches, street and campus evangelism, and courses in the city's Free University. During the fall of 1972, the front also started "The Crucible"—a forum for radical (but Orthodox) Christian studies, meeting at CWLF's headquarters house just east of Telegraph Avenue on the south side of the UC campus. Regular courses included at the opening: (1) A History of the Radical Church—Donatists, Anabaptists, Quakers, and others, to twentieth-century Christian radicals; (2) The Androclean Forum—important questions raised by participants concerning radical Christianity in a "post-Christian" world; (3) Women's Liberation in the Context of Radical Christianity; and (4) Introduction to New Testament Greek. Saturday "mini-courses" consisted of: (1) God's Great Pledge—the idea of covenant in the Old and New Testaments; and (2) Evil and Punishment—a study of C. S. Lewis's *The Great Divorce.* All of these courses and mini-courses were to be supplemented by occasional public meetings dealing with relevant contemporary problems.

Second, CWLF translates its social concern into action by providing medical service to street people, distributing food and clothing to the needy—especially those in the drug culture—and maintaining several

"Jesus houses" for addicts trying to kick the habit. The front also supports an agricultural commune in the hills of southern Humboldt County—The House of the Rising Son—a group of counterculture Christians seeking to develop a back-to-the-land alternative life-style based upon a rich understanding of discipleship. Furthermore, in 1972, CWLF conducted a ministry of evangelism and compassion at the Democratic and Republican conventions at Miami Beach, where the brothers and sisters camped with the various protestors at Flamingo Park and witnessed to their faith in Christ.

Third, and possibly the most innovative attempt undertaken by the front, CWLF established in 1969 a monthly "underground" Christian newspaper—*Right On*—the first of over fifty which have since emerged around the world. During 1971, and again very recently, the *Right On* staff was reorganized and professionalized with Jack Sparks as publisher and Sharon Gallagher as editor. (Ms. Gallagher is a graduate of Westmont College and comes out of the Plymouth Brethren.) *Right On*'s literary style is well conceived. Its eight or more pages include book reviews, letters, cartoons, editorials, coverage of local events, as well as articles dealing with religious, educational, social, and political topics relevant to students and street people in the greater San Francisco Bay area, where CWLF distributes the newspaper free.

Although the front is not connected with any one church or denomination, it does receive financial and other support from various Evangelical churches, such as the affluent First Presbyterian Church of Berkeley. Some CWLF brothers and sisters are "into" the institutional church; others are not. And despite the fact that the front has no interest in numbers, it is now clearly one of the most effective ministries of any kind in this notorious city of northern California.

Perhaps the best summary of CWLF's purpose for existence is reflected in the conclusion of Sharon Gallagher's report in the September 1972 issue of *Right On*, concerning the Family's experience ministering to the various protest groups camped in Miami Beach's Flamingo Park during the 1972 political conventions:

Thursday morning the Family passed out bananas and orange juice in the park to people who were packing up, some of whom had just gotten out of jail. After driving a woman to jail who needed to contact a friend, we passed the park in the afternoon and it was deserted. It was all so serene it seemed like it all never happened.

But we had been there, slept there, worshipped there, saw new brothers and sisters born into the Family. We had loved people there.

Where will all that energy go now? One man who had been at all the major rallies for years said that this was probably the last of the major demonstrations. Where would the people go? Home to smoke dope and listen to records? . . .

We left Miami Beach with our hearts heavy for what we had seen there, the hatred and fear, with a new awareness of our call to be peacemakers, our responsibilities to speak to the issues of life (page 11).

Leighton Ford, Inter-Varsity Christian Fellowship, and Christian World Liberation Front are three prominent exponents of the new kind of evangelism exposed by the Young Evangelicals—one that meets the needs of the *whole* person. It should come as no surprise to anyone that much of this evangelism is indeed campus-oriented. After all, college and university communities attract not only young people who are technically undergraduates or graduate students, they also provide one of the few environments where alienated youth—street people—can find some measure of social acceptance.

At this point, we should note that campus ministry and evangelism is one of the more strikingly successful dimensions of the current Evangelical renaissance. Its increasing effectiveness in numerous forms and styles of ministry is apparent almost everywhere. At the same time, mainstream Ecumenical Liberal campus ministries have been declining already for several years. While Liberal Protestant campus pastors have taken a seemingly ever more secular stance and have even eliminated their once regular services of worship for students, their own denominations have seen fit to cut their financial support of what appears to them an increasingly fruitless type of ministry. In seeking to uphold and identify with the radical secular student movements, Liberal campus ministers have failed to provide a solid biblical-theological foundation for such activity—one that might well be expected by the supporting ecclesiastical bodies. Even churches located in college and university communities which previously backed the interdenominational United Ministries in Higher Education are withdrawing their financial aid. For example, Cary Weisiger III, Pastor of the Menlo Park Presbyterian

Church in Menlo Park, California, indicates the depth of the problem
faced by his own mainline church in an article which appeared in the
March 30, 1973 edition of *Christianity Today*:

> We have changed. In the last decade, for example, we have felt the impact
> of student revolt at nearby colleges and universities, and we have reacted against
> what we felt was an incredible compromise and weakness on the part of inter-
> denominational ministries at those places. When one of the campus ministers
> at a neighboring university finally stated that he was a Marxist, a Leninist, and
> a Maoist, he was let go by the interdenominational board not because he was
> ideologically unacceptable but for "lack of funds." Our governing board had
> discontinued program support two years before (p. 685).

Yet, at the same time, some of the socially concerned mainline
churches in campus communities are finding the ministries of the
Young Evangelicals a better alternative for their support. These
churches are attracted by the strength and life-transforming power of
the Young Evangelical witness. They find it refreshing to encounter
completely changed students and street people who have kicked the
drug habit, who are honestly trying to love their neighbor and bring the
mandates of biblical faith to bear on the pressing social ills of the present
day. Perhaps the mainstream Ecumenical Liberal campus ministries
could learn something worthwhile from their Young Evangelical counterparts.

We have now discussed new priorities of the Young Evangelicals
stemming out of two basic areas of concern: (1) the development of a
richer understanding of the inspiration and authority of Scripture as a
basis for action in the world; and (2) the mandate for evangelism as the
proclamation of the Gospel in its entirety—relevant to the whole person
and all his needs. A third general area of concern in their thinking is the
life of discipleship—discovering the values appropriate to the transformed life in Christ. We shall now take a close look at the priorities
emerging from the Young Evangelicals' fresh understanding of the
meaning of Christian discipleship.

C. EVANGELICAL SOCIAL GOSPEL

It would be unfair to say that contemporary Fundamentalists or Establishment Evangelicals have not felt at least some obligation to come to the aid of the downtrodden and helpless in society. But the Young Evangelicals believe that their churches' admirable attempt to relieve the short-term suffering of individuals—through food and clothing collections, rescue missions, and the like—is merely treating the symptoms rather than *curing* the disease itself. In order to treat social ills in even a *relatively* democratic society, the proper use of political power and economic pressure by persons and groups is a virtual necessity. Modern Orthodoxy, however, has generally maintained that social action—especially when the issues involved are political in nature—is a matter for individual Christians, not churches or demonstrations corporately. Thus, Establishment Evangelical and Fundamentalist churches feel they are abiding by the principle of separation of church and state. Reacting against this hypocritical stance, the Young Evangelicals point out that Orthodox denominations and churches which criticize Liberal religious bodies for their political activities are themselves often quite willing to act in the same way when the preservation of the status quo is at stake. These young men and women would also suggest that the doctrine of separation of church and state has, in fact, been misinterpreted, that it really pertains to the prohibition of government interference in church affairs and does not forbid the churches to speak and act prophetically when the state fosters political or social unrighteousness.

We have already seen that the Young Evangelicals are manifesting new priorities based upon the conviction that positive social concern and action are as much a part of the Gospel as personal salvation—they are reverse sides of the same coin. Furthermore, these young men and women also reject their churches' adherence to a personal and social ethic which they claim is rooted in Scripture but is, in fact, grounded much more in (1) antiquated social mores and the cultural baggage of revivalism, (2) civil religion and the American Way of Life, and (3) a harsh legalism contrary to the spirit of the New Testament itself.

One of the most articulate spokesmen within the Evangelical community for the integral relationship between the personal and the social dimensions of Christian faith is David Moberg, formerly professor of sociology at Bethel College (Baptist General Conference), St. Paul, Minnesota, and now chairman of the Department of Sociology and Anthropology at Marquette University. Through his classic text in the sociology of religion—*The Church as a Social Institution*—Moberg has made the "functional" study of religion acceptable to Evangelicals who once regarded sociology and religion as incompatible disciplines.

Recently, the highly respected sociologist and former member of the Evangelicals for McGovern Committee wrote a book from the sociological perspective on traditional evangelism and contemporary social action —*The Great Reversal: Evangelism versus Social Concern* (Phila. and N.Y.: Lippincott, 1972). Here Moberg suggests that prior to the Social Gospel movement and the subsequent Fundamentalist–Modernist controversy, social concern and evangelism tended to go hand in hand. To prove his point, the sociologist cites the work of such eminent Evangelical Christians of the past as Charles G. Finney, F. B. Meyer, John H. Jowett, Charles H. Spurgeon, and T. de Witt Talmadge. But with the rise of the Social Gospel and the Fundamentalist–Modernist debate, polarization has taken place within American Protestantism, and Orthodoxy has, by and large, *changed* its course from a socially concerned evangelism to personal evangelism alone. This change, then, is the "Great Reversal."

To begin, Moberg feels that the ethics of Americanism and Christian faith are contrary:

The typical Christian is a "good American" in his political behavior. He acts upon the American principle that each person and group ought to seek its own goals and, as each does so, out of it all will emerge a consensus for action that will constitute the greatest good for the greatest number. To put it very crassly in moralistic words, selfishness is the root principle of our political system.

Americans selfishly assume that whatever is best for their own subculture, their own occupational group, their own neighborhood, city, state, or county, will obviously be best for the entire nation—indeed, for the entire world. The definition of "what is best" generally is along economic lines.

This perspective is in strong contrast to New Testament ethics which declare that we should love one another, put the interests of others ahead of our own selfish striving, bear one another's burdens, do good to all men, and even love our enemies and bless those who despitefully use us (pp. 126–127).

He then goes on to chide the typical negativism and social unconcern of Evangelicals who more than other Christians identify the cross with the flag:

In regard to most social issues of this century, evangelicals are known for their negative positions—what they are against—rather than for a positive stand. They have worked for changed lives of individuals but not for changes in society, except as these might incidentally occur through converts. At the same time, they have described social conditions as going from bad to worse without recognizing that their own lack of social action to correct the structural evils of society and their professed "neutrality," which in reality constituted support of the power structure, were major factors contributing to the deterioration of social conditions (p. 177).

The sum of Moberg's argument is that the Great Reversal must be reversed. He says, "The fracturing impact of polarized thinking that compels Christians to believe that they must be either *activists*, who attack entrenched social evils, or *pietists*, who emphasize the life of prayer, worship, devotion, and personal evangelism, can be overcome only by the realization that both perspectives are important. Pietism and activism are interdependent. Pietism is the root of the Christian life and activism its fruit" (p. 153). The sociologist concludes by describing the fresh political and social concerns of the Young Evangelicals as good evidence that Orthodoxy is indeed being transformed. He declares, finally, that

evangelicals are awakening to their inconsistencies and returning to the totality of the Christian gospel. As a result, the old dichotomies between salvation and service, changing lives and changing society, proclamation and demonstration, man's vertical and horizontal relationships, personal piety and social service, faith and works, and believing and loving, all of which can be summed up in relationship to the contrast between evangelism and social concern, are breaking down (pp. 177–178).

It is in this spirit that the Young Evangelicals espouse a truly Evangelical Social Gospel—one that meets the deepest needs of the heart and the urgent demands of a society in turmoil as well. Their new values and ethics—motivated by a biblical faith and a rich understanding of the meaning of discipleship—are best reflected in the fresh priorities of these young men and women which include: (1) sexual love as a joyful experience; (2) meaningful interpersonal and social relationships and the dignity of women; (3) racial justice; (4) the politics of conscience; (5) the fight against poverty; (6) a healthy natural environment; and (7) a positive and happy participation in contemporary culture.

1. Sexual Love as a Joyful Experience: Bruce Larson

The monstrosity of sexual intercourse outside marriage is that those who indulge in it are trying to isolate one kind of union (the sexual) from all the other kinds of union which were intended to go along with it and make up the total union. The Christian attitude does not mean that there is anything wrong about sexual pleasure, any more than about the pleasure of eating. It means that you must not isolate that pleasure and try to get it by itself, any more than you ought to try to get the pleasures of taste without swallowing and digesting, by chewing things and spitting them out again.

C. S. Lewis,
Mere Christianity

Here we *are*—there really are men like us, with a certain peculiarity in our make-up which is in itself no more morally blameworthy than left-handedness. We are *not* necessarily pansies, or bohemians, or maniacs, or lechers. Many of us do our best to lead decent respectable lives and to appear as normal human beings, and some of us succeed. And so long as our abnormal affections are never expressed in ways which are against the law, whether God's law or man's, the law speaks nothing against us. So why should an ignorant society? Why should a Pharisaic church?

Alex Davidson,
The Returns of Love

The church has all but closed its doors to millions of people in America whose only difference from the majority is their sexual orientation. Homosexuals want to be a part of the church of the Lord Jesus Christ, as happy individuals, as "born again" believers, and as individuals who can hold their heads high without shame. The church only can make that possible.

Troy Perry,
Is Gay Good?

Orthodox Christians enjoy sex too—but they are too often afraid to admit it. Evangelicals and Fundamentalists—many of them—adhere to a kind of gnosticism (one of the earliest and most dangerous heresies—rebuffed by Paul in Colossians) in which matter in general and the flesh in particular are inherently bad, and only the spirit is good. Sex, therefore, becomes for them something hardly better than a necessary evil.

Orthodox Christians also have their own sexual mythology. They delude themselves into an implicit belief that for the believer, sex really does not begin until marriage—and then only in the "missionary position." These same Fundamentalists and Evangelicals fail to realize that *every* pubescent and post-pubescent male or female, married or single, Christian or non-Christian, has a sex life which may include one or more of the following: (1) sexual fantasies, (2) "wet dreams," (3) masturbation, (4) heterosexual intercourse, and (5) homosexual activity. Moreover, such Christians would be wise to consider whether the moral legalism demanded by some of their own churches—forbidding social dancing, attendance at the theater, even mixed bathing—might serve to increase rather than prevent promiscuity. For in those churches, frustrated young people often find that necking, petting, and their natural results constitute the *only* forms of social entertainment—apart from church or sport, perhaps—open to them. And they are quick to take advantage of such pursuits—right under the watchful (yet sometimes blinded) eyes of their pastor and parents. Orthodoxy, therefore, needs to demythologize sex. Sexual myths and unrealistic personal ethics not only inhibit growth and fulfillment, they also give rise both to hypocrisy and to self-righteousness. Hypocrisy for those who cannot—or will not—meet the standards imposed upon them, but dare not admit it. Self-righteousness for those who fulfill the demands and are eager to expose those who do not. Furthermore, given the effectiveness and availability of contraception and treatment of venereal disease, easy divorce, and the permissive society in general, the old sexual taboos espoused by Orthodox Christianity are harder to enforce. So, it is high time for Evangelical Christians to thoughtfully reappraise their traditional views regarding human sexuality.

Surely one of the most enlightened yet *biblical* demythologizers of sex today is Bruce Larson, a Presbyterian minister and leader of Group Research and Individual Leadership. In his book, *Ask Me to Dance* (Waco, Texas: Word Books, 1972), this Evangelical thinker discusses sex not as an entity unto itself but as one dimension of life which cannot be separated from the other aspects of human personality. Accepting the fact that Orthodoxy does hold sexual myths that need to be exploded, Larson maintains, "There is no one who needs to be more enlightened about sex than those of us who have had a Christian upbringing" (page 91). At the same time, enlightenment for him means getting at an authentic Christian sex ethic appropriate for the present time, rather than merely adopting the morality of the permissive society or sinking again into another form of legalism. Thus, on the one hand, he rejects the notion that sex is simply a necessary evil, that the body is inherently bad, that celibacy is preferable to marriage, and on the other hand, that sex is just a biological function meant to be enjoyed—if it feels good, do it. Instead, Larson puts forward a third alternative, "that sex is good and to be enjoyed but always in the context of responsibility. Christians ought to be sexy. Sex is not a necessary evil but a gift given by God to enjoy. God has also given certain rules that make us responsible for others and for ourselves. Within these confines, sex is a powerful and wonderful gift to be celebrated" (p. 93). What he means by this is not that Orthodox Christianity should *relinquish* genuinely biblical principles regulating sexual activity, but that it must separate these legitimate rules from the *unbiblical* cultural trappings that became a part of Christian sex ethics in the Puritan and Victorian past. From the Young Evangelical perspective, Larson demythologizes five particularly important areas of sexual activity or human states in which sex is a significant factor. These are masturbation, premarital sex, sex in marriage, extramarital sex and divorce, and homosexuality.

First, he completely dismisses as false the old belief that masturbation is in itself physically or mentally harmful or both. Larson contends, in fact, that "masturbation can be the way God has given for easing what seems like intolerable tension, both for the single and the married" (p. 100). At the same time, however, he states that it can also be "a way of literally taking your destiny in your own hands" (p. 100)—of not allowing God to provide for your sexuality. Thus, the Presbyterian minister is really arguing that solo sex is not bad, not immoral, but, since sex is intended for two, it is clearly not God's best.

Second, Larson deals with the area of premarital sex. Given the fact that science has virtually removed the two chief threats of pregnancy and veneral disease as a consequence of intercourse, he maintains that we must find a genuinely biblical approach to the problem that will say yes or no on some other basis than the possibility of disease or unwanted pregnancy. And in this connection, Larson does come out on the conservative side. For the Bible teaches "that any time two people have intercourse, these two people become one in body, mind, and spirit. Far from being dirty or evil, sex at the point of intercourse is so powerful that you become one with another person. The obvious implication is that one cannot have this experience with many people, or even with several people, without violating himself as well as the other" (p. 95).

This seems to be an implicit case for premarital chastity. In other words, fulfillment in intercourse demands a lasting bond of commitment between a man and a woman—one so authentic and sincere that it does not shy away from the marriage vows which seal that commitment in the eyes of society.

Third, the Presbyterian minister talks about sex *in* marriage, where his phrase "sexy Christians" takes on special meaning. For instance, what about *positions* permissible for lovemaking? Larson contends here "that there is no position that two people can use in making love that is off limits except where one of the persons feels violated or imposed upon or embarrassed. . . . We do the thing that will bring fulfillment to the other " (p. 96). Thus, God does not in any way regulate the marriage bed. Neither does he require that a woman become a mere tool or convenience for the satisfaction of her husband in intercourse. She has just as much right to sexual fulfillment as he does.

Fourth, the Young Evangelical discusses extramarital sex and the tragedy of divorce. Larson feels that because adultery specifically violates one of the Ten Commandments—God's law—it is a more serious offense against him than premarital intercourse. In the traditional Christian view, unfaithfulness is like cutting into a living organism made one flesh in the bond of marriage. Therefore, adultery is actually more than just breaking a pledge. It is a violation of the wholeness of two persons' humanity. Nevertheless, the Presbyterian minister is quick to chide those who have blown extramarital sex out of all proportion "until it has become 'the unforgivable sin.' We feel much less strongly about coveting or not honoring your father and mother, for example. This commandment must be seen in proportion with the other nine" (p. 97). How many pastors and committed lay leaders in Orthodox churches have been deprived of their positions and are marked for the rest of their lives in those same churches for *one* sexual mistake, or even for one sin alleged but not proven? It is strange that such a situation should develop in a community of faith where the power and presence of sin are always taken seriously. How many times are we to forgive our brother? At this point, the Young Evangelicals wonder where the Christian virtues of forgiveness and charity have gone—when the unforgivable sin (in the eyes of the self-righteous) has been committed.

In treating the dissolution of marriage, Larson admits that Scripture is clear on the wrongness of divorce. But he also reminds us that sometimes we are forced to choose the lesser of two evils. What, then, should be done when a Christian man and his Christian wife no longer can live together *creatively?* Here the Presbyterian minister takes what in traditional Orthodoxy is a controversial stand:

It may be that divorce is a way out for both. To stay married for the sake of the children does irreparable harm to the children and there is no justification for that. To stay married in order to fulfill some law of God that destroys people is no law of God. And even though it is not what God planned for man, it may be better than staying married to someone you wish were dead, for that is murder, or imagining that you are married to someone else, for that is adultery (p. 97).

Finally, Bruce Larson takes up the very complex issue of homosexuality. In this discussion, he maintains that much of this problem lies in our assignment of *arbitrary* male and female roles to individuals. What he means is that we should stop assuming that a boy who is by nature aesthetic or artistic or gentle is therefore not a man. Likewise, we ought not suppose that a girl who is aggressive or a good manager or a natural organizer is therefore less than female or even masculine. A man may feel so ashamed of being "effeminate" that he stops competing with men and implicitly enters the female world. The same, of course, can be true vice versa for a woman.

For Larson, homosexuality (whether a form of learned behavior or not) is abnormal in the sense that it is not what God intended for a whole person. But he rebukes Christians for their outright condemnation of men and women whose only difference from the majority is sexual orientation, arguing that they should love them, show concern for them, and help them whenever possible enter some kind of heterosexual life where fulfillment can be realized. In this connection, the Presbyterian minister claims that he knows no homosexual who is really happy. On the surface, he says, a man or woman may shout, "Gay is groovy!" but underneath it is a long, hard, and lonely road.

Homosexuals may well be the most persecuted minority in America. And the Church must share the blame for that persecution. At the same time, contemporary Evangelical thinkers *have* softened their stand by making the distinction between homosexual *orientation* and *practice*. Only the latter, they feel, warrants disapproval on the basis of Scripture. Carl Henry sounds very much like Bruce Larson in this regard: "The church of Christ must never forget that the homosexual has little disposition to seek help while he associates only with his 'queer' cohorts. Only the opening of new avenues of acquaintance and fellowship initiated from the side of the heterosexual world can be the first introduction to a therapeutic community."[10] Yet, the fact of the matter is that most (perhaps almost all) Evangelicals and Fundamentalists fail to distinguish between homosexual orientation and practice. Thus, to ask the gay person to be honest about his condition in the company of his Christian kindred is to ask him to accept social ostracism, whether or not he is willing to refrain from homosexual activity and seek therapy. For, by and large, Fundamentalists and Evangelicals refuse to accept the gay person on the grounds that whatever attempt at rehabilitation he may undertake could be unsuccessful. Therefore, his continued presence in their church constitutes a bad influence at best and a danger at worst (but why any more than a heterosexual?). Especially sad, of course, is the homosexual pastor or seminarian who admits his condition (the clergy as a profession has always attracted numerous homosexuals). Most likely, such admission would mean the end of his ministerial career. Where again, ask the Young Evangelicals, are the classic Christian virtues of forgiveness and charity Orthodoxy claims it holds so dear?

One significant outcome of Orthodox Christianity's rejection of the homosexual as a person has been the establishment throughout the U.S. and Canada of gay Metropolitan Community Churches (MCC) in urban areas where homosexuals tend to congregate. Banded together in a newly formed denomination, these churches adhere to a statement of faith similar in content to that of the National Association of Evangelicals, and emphasize personal conversion and traditional evangelism. But they also engage in meaningful social action to ease the burdens inherent within the gay community itself. This is one case in which the reality of discrimination and persecution on the home front has *forced* churches to serve their communities by a concrete social witness.

In 1968, Troy Perry, a graduate of Moody Bible Institute and a former Pentecostal minister, founded the MCC mother church in Los Angeles. Unlike some of his mainstream Ecumenical Liberal counterparts, Perry *has* made an honest attempt to find a biblical justification for homosexual life and practice. And the leaflet published by the board of elders of the Universal Fellowship of Metropolitian Community Churches, *Homosexuality: What the Bible Does . . . and Does Not Say!*, discusses and reinterprets all Old and New Testament references (and alleged references) to homosexuality. It concludes its (perhaps strained) exegesis by saying that, at least in the New Testament, only homosexual activity motivated by *lust* is really condemned. Thus, MCC argues that gay persons, like heterosexual couples, should be allowed to form lasting "marital" relationships—sanctioned by law and the Church—which would tend to prevent the promiscuous sexual encounters now characteristic of the gay life-style.

Nevertheless, the MCC stance leaves certain issues concerning homosexuality unresolved. First, it is yet to be demonstrated that the gay life as a whole is either happy or fulfilled. Gaydom seems anything but gay. Homosexuals maintain that their sorrows are merely caused by the disaproval and persecution of the wider society against them—*not* because there is something inherently *wrong* with their condition. But is this, in fact, the case? Second, at least among males, raw sex appears to be the single most important aspect of homosexual life. Youth, attractiveness, and genital size ("endowment") become key factors in the successful gay love life. A homosexual male is generally an "old man" before he reaches 30; after that, it is downhill all the way. Finally, male homosexuals, anyway, are known for their very frequent change of partners and one-night stands, and the relative *difficulty* they experience in forming permanent relationships with one partner, the absence of legal sanction notwithstanding. Homosexual couples do not grow old gracefully together.

Hence, most "straight" (heterosexual) Young Evangelicals would probably take the position of Bruce Larson over the one espoused by Troy Perry and the Metropolitan Community Churches. But they realize that there are no pat answers to the problem of homosexuality. For one thing, these young men and women repudiate the widespread notion in Orthodoxy that conversion to Christ is the solution *alone*—any more than it is the *simple* answer to the oppression caused by racial injustice, poverty, or chronic illness. The existence of the MCC's and their Evangelical members proves otherwise. Nevertheless, conversion itself might indeed provide a homosexual with motivation to change (something absoultely necessary for successful psychiatric therapy) *if* it is accompanied, as Carl Henry suggests, by the positive reinforcement of a caring, loving, and therapeutic community. Are the churches willing?

Human sexuality as a joyful experience related to personal wholeness, then, is a manifest new priority of the Young Evangelicals. By demythologizing sex in the context of biblical principles, moreover, they are operating in marked contrast to their mainstream Ecumenical Liberal counterparts who have increasingly accepted situation ethics with its one, vaguely interpreted norm—love. Thus, in the eyes of those Liberals, the Young Evangelicals probably appear conservative in their attitudes toward sex. Such an appraisal may be true. But within their own tradition, the Young Evangelicals are radical, because in condemning sin they insist on *not* condemning the sinner. These young men and women recognize the obligation always to accept, love, and forgive as a way of life. And that is what is clearly revolutionary about the sex ethics of the Young Evangelicals.

2. Neither Male Nor Female: Meaningful Interpersonal and Social Relationships

> I remember reading about a black girl who moved here from Angola in West Africa. Her name was Maria and she was always laughing. One day she went to a meeting on evangelism in her church where they were talking about pamphlets, missions, campaigns, and all the rest. At one point someone turned to Maria and said, "What do they do in your church in Angola, Maria?" "In my church," said Maria, after a moment's thought, "we don't give pamphlets to people or have missions. We just send one or two

Christian families to live in a village. And when people see what Christians are like, then they want to be Christians themselves." It seems to me that this simplicity and artlessness is the key to evangelism in the church.

Bruce Larson, *Ask Me to Dance*

In Jesus there are no niggers' or 'whiteys,' no 'freaks' or 'straights, no male or female because we are all one in Him. If we belong to Jesus, then we're the true children of Abraham and members of the forever family, just like the promise said.

Galatians 3:28, 29 *(Letters to Street Christians)*

Perhaps it is no wonder that the women were first at the Cradle and last at the Cross. They had never known a man like this man —there never has been such another. A prophet and teacher who never nagged at them, never flattered or coaxed or patronised; who never made arch jokes about them, never treated them either as "The women, God help us!" or "The Ladies, God bless them!" who rebuked without querulousness and praised without conde- scension; who took their questions and arguments seriously; who never mapped out their sphere for them, never urged them to be feminine or jeered at them for being female; who had no axe to grind and no uneasy male dignity to defend; who took them as he found them and was completely unself-conscious. There is no act, no sermon, no parable in the whole Gospel that borrows its pun- gency from female perversity; nobody could possibly guess from the words and deeds of Jesus that there was anything "funny" about woman's nature.

Dorothy Sayers, *Are Women Human?*

The widespread popularity in Evangelical circles of Dr. Thomas A. Harris's book, *I'm O.K.; You're O.K.*, should come as a surprise to no one. For despite much talk about love, fellowship, and acceptance on the part of Fundamentalist and Evangelical churches, very little of these qualities actually goes into practice within institutional Orthodoxy. Doc- trinal rigidity, ethical legalism, and the stringent qualifications for lead- ership tend together to result in self-righteousness and excessive role- playing among members of Orthodox churches. Those who are honest about their doctrinal disagreement with the stated position of a church are not loved even if *they* are loving persons. Those who fail to live up to all the ethical demands—often conditioned more by culture than Scripture—are denied full fellowship. And no one is really accepted "just as I am." Failure to live up to expectations as a member of an Evangelical or Fundamentalist congregation bars a layperson or pastor from assuming or continuing in church leadership; and so often in Orthodoxy, only those who are leaders in their church enjoy *complete* acceptance by the brethren. The doctrine of separation from the world characteristic of Orthodox Christianity encourages the development of the church as the Christian's country club. But since that church *technically* has open membership subject only to doctrinal agreement, confession of faith, and assent to ethical standards, the real possibility of discrimination within the church surfaces only *after* a person joins the congregation.

This is not the New Testament pattern. Jesus himself associated and identified with sinners—with the poor, the outcasts, and those who held no standing within the synagogue or the wider society. The Church as the Body of Christ and the community of faith should be the one place where *every* man and woman can feel at home—where the stranger finds that he is accepted with his strengths and weaknesses, but more than that, where he finds love as someone created in the image of God, someone for whom Christ died. The Church ought to be the place where a man or woman is challenged and encouraged to receive new life, to become a disciple of Jesus Christ—but also the place where he is forgiven when he fails. It must be a community in which an individual can be honest about who he is, his hopes, aspirations, and hurts.

An increasing number of progressive Evangelical churches are indeed striving for better and more meaningful interpersonal relationships among their members through sensitivity training, "group encounter" weekends, Transactional Analysis (T.A.), nonverbal forms of communication (hand-holding, embracing, dancing, and the like) even in worship, and small groups for study, fellowship, prayer, and worship-celebration. Utilizing these methods, they are also encouraging their members to be honest and open about their day-to-day problems. Thus, the church functions as a therapeutic community, applying the principle of Christian, self-sacrificing love to the demands inherent in meeting the concrete emotional needs of men and women.

The Young Evangelicals welcome this new theology of relationships, not only for the sake of Christian "insiders," but also for the sake of the world. They know that committed Christians who can relate to un-believers in a spirit of genine concern, love, and openness are far more likely to be effective witnesses than those Christians who merely feel an *obligation* to witness and "get down to business" as soon as possible, by direct confrontation (e.g., door-to-door or on the street), distribution of tracts, and other such methods. In this connection, Fuller Theological Seminary requires a program of sensitivity training of all students, while Bruce Larson's work fosters church renewal by facilitating the develop-ment and growth of relationship theology in individual congregations so to promote deeper fellowship and better evangelism.

Besides confronting the problem of meaningful interpersonal rela-tionships among believers per se, Orthodoxy has yet to take its women seriously with respect to their status in society in general and their standing in the Church in particular. That woman is inferior to man is an established doctrine in most Fundamentalist and Evangelical churches. Countering this assumption, Nancy Hardesty, a Young Evan-gelical who teaches English at Trinity College (Evangelical Free Church of America), Deerfield, Illinois, offers a fresh interpretation of the role of women in marriage in Pauline theology in *The Cross & The Flag* (Robert G. Clouse, Robert D. Linder, Richard V. Pierard, eds. Carol Stream, Illinois: Creation House, 1972):

Perhaps the most quoted passage on marriage is found in Ephesians 5. Unfortu-nately most commentators begin with verse 22 ("Wives, submit yourselves unto your own husbands") rather than at verse 21 ("submitting yourselves one to another in the fear of God"), where the thought logically begins. Throughout the passage Paul is describing the mutual, self-giving, *agape* love and unity that should characterize Christ's church. Wives should love and work with their husbands as the church does with Christ; husbands should love and sacrifice themselves for their wives as Christ gave His life for the church. Paul is not setting up a hierarchical relationship here or encouraging men to think of themselves as playing God to their wives. Rather, he is encouraging all Chris-tians to conform to Christ. Wherever the New Testament speaks of the mar-riage relationship (Col. 3:18–19; I Cor. 11:11–12; I Pet. 3:1, 7), both husband and wife are addressed and both are admonished to love and submit to one another. The relationship is always seen as reciprocal.

Young couples today who seek a companionate, partnership marriage should not feel that they are disobeying God's Word by not forcing the wife to submit or the husband to carry the entire load of decisions (p. 75).

On the issue of the woman's function in the Church, Nancy Hardesty also offers a new interpretation of the Pauline passages of Scripture in which the Apostle supposedly teaches silence on the part of women in the Church:

The other question is whether or not women should keep silence in church as they are supposedly commanded in I Corinthians 14:34 and I Timothy 2:11. Both of these, along with I Corinthians 11:1–15, are extremely difficult passages to interpret. Involved are arguments concerning Genesis that seem to rely more heavily on Jewish tradition than the Old Testament. They also seem to contradict the practice of the church as recorded in Acts and other epistles. Particularly in I Corinthians, Paul seems to be primarily concerned with custom, with maintaining church decorum, with having things done decently and in order (14:10).

Various interpretations of these passages have been put forward. . . .

Perhaps the most helpful is the solution worked out by Russell Prohl in *Woman in the Church*. He found evidence throughout the New Testament that services were divided between a preliminary service at which inquirers were present to hear what the gospel was all about and a closed meeting held afterward in which only baptized Christians celebrated holy communion. Those passages commanding women to be silent appear to deal with the open meeting, during which the church was trying to impress and convince nonbelievers. Women being in a low position in that society, unbelievers might have been shocked and turned away by women teaching. However, in the service of holy communion (I Cor. 11:20–34), women were permitted to preach and prophesy (I Cor. 11:5). Paul's primary concern there was that women should retain the symbol of their marriage, lest even believers be misled into thinking that Christianity was destroying the family (pp. 76–77).

Ironically, when we look at Jesus himself, he hardly appears to have been a male chauvinist. The Gospels offer no evidence that Jesus ever treated women as inferior to men. This was in marked contrast to the restricted state of women in Palestinian Judaism at the time. For instance, women were not entrusted with the words of the Torah; they were not counted toward a quorum for worship; they could not bear witness. A proper man (certainly a rabbi) would not speak to a woman in public; and a menstruating woman was considered ritually unclean as was anything she touched.

But Jesus addressed women publicly—even women of ill repute—and spoke to them as human beings rather than sex objects (e.g., the thrice-married Samaritan woman, the woman taken in adultery, and Mary Magdalene). He taught women the Torah. Jesus deliberately repudiated the Jewish prohibition against women bearing witness. His first resurrection appearance was to a woman he commissioned to bear witness to the Eleven. Jesus rejected the ancient blood taboo by publicly healing the woman with a twelve-year issue of blood and not shrinking from the ritual uncleanness incurred by that act. Furthermore, he demonstrated that the intellectual life is not restricted to men, nor is the place of women necessarily in the home, as was pointed out in the summer, 1972 issue of *The Post-American* (in a reprint of an article which originally appeared in *The Boston Globe*):

> This was made clear during his visit to the home of Martha and Mary. Martha took the typical women's role: "Martha was distracted with much serving." Mary, however, took the supposedly "male" role: she "sat at the Lord's feet and listened to his teaching." Martha apparently thought Mary was out of place in choosing the role of the "intellectual," for she complained to Jesus. But Jesus' response was a refusal to force all women into the stereotype: he treated Mary first of all as a person (whose highest faculty is the intellect, the spirit) who was allowed to set her own priorities, and in this instance had "chosen the better part." And Jesus applauded her: "it is not to be taken from her" (p. 11).

Thus Jesus vigorously promoted the equality and dignity of women even in the midst of a male-dominated society. Yet, as the *New York Times* once suggested, "Churches are one of the few important institutions that still elevate discrimination against women to the level of principle" (quoted in *The Cross & The Flag*, p. 77). In a day when America is finally beginning to liberate her female citizens, why does the Church continue to resist? The Young Evangelicals believe that their churches should give equal representation to women on their governing boards, in the ministry (where their salaries should equal those given to men), and in denominational and interdenominational hierarchies where female executives are most rarely encountered. Women's Liberation is here to stay, and once again Orthodoxy is dragging its feet.

3. Racial Justice: Tom Skinner

23 Psalm of the Black Man

The white man has been my shepherd. I have always been in want.

He maketh me to lie down on welfare and poverty. He leadeth me into the noisy, rat-infested ghetto. He despieseth my soul.

He leadeth me into the field of inhuman labor for his profit's sake. Yea, when we toiled through the sea and cotton fields of death, he was doing no evil for he said God was with him.

Thy whip and thy chain discomfort me. Thou preparest a table before me on television in the presence of my hungry children.

Thou anointest my head with self-hatred and bitterness. My cup runneth over.

Surely, the fight for liberation and equality shall drive me all the days of my life, and we shall dwell in the house of freedom some day.

Donald Oden,
The Other Side

Among all the social ills of modern America, racial injustice has perhaps received the most attention in Evangelical circles. Both Evangelicals and Open Fundamentalists—following the characteristic "me too" pattern—are now vocally condemning racism *in principle.* Yet, 11 AM Sunday is still the most segregated hour of the week. Why? Because the institutional church is Orthodoxy's country club where Christians get together with "their own kind." But even apart from the fact that their churches remain, by and large, segregated, Fundamentalists and Evangelicals have been among the last to approve practical social, political, and legal measures to combat racial injustice in the wider society— busing and integration of schools in general, affirmative action in employment, desegregation of middle-class suburban neighborhoods, and the like. Hence, the lily-white churches and the sociopolitical inaction or reaction of Evangelicals and Open Fundamentalists demonstrate the hypocrisy of their pious words.

In recent years, a number of Young Evangelicals from the Black community have begun to voice strong criticism of their white brothers and sisters in Evangelical churches because of that self-evident hypocrisy. Among these young men and women is Columbus Salley, co-author with Ronald Behm of *Your God Is Too White* (Downers Grove, Ill.; Intervarsity Press, 1970), a blistering attack on Evangelical racism, based upon biblical principles, historical evidence, contemporary social realities, and the positive elements of Black Power. Salley and his white co-author conclude their argument against allegiance to an all-white God by urging their Evangelical brothers and sisters to "De-honkify (de-whiten) your church: its curriculum, its investment and purchasing programs, its leadership and its attitudes" (p. 114). Once *churches* are truly integrated and Blacks and whites get to know each other in worship, prayer, and fellowship as coequals under the lordship of Christ, those same whites will be motivated not only to approve of racial equality under the law but also to fight for it.

Another persuasive critic of the hypocrisy of white Evangelicals is Black Evangelist William Pannell, an associate of Tom Skinner and a trustee of Fuller Theological Seminary. Pannell demands that Evangelicals repudiate the traditional Christ of white, suburban America and its civil religion in favor of the universal, risen Lord Jesus Christ who liberates and reconciles an oppressed humanity:

> Whatever God says today must be expressed in intelligible, concrete acts of compassion that "vibrate with relevance to all conditions of men." This is incarnational living; this is "fleshing out the words we profess."
>
> Here we clearly need to preach a Christ who moves alongside of contemporary man, helping him to affirm his individuality and personal worth. Unfortunately, He often comes through as Anglo-Saxon, Protestant, suburban, Republican. Black young people simply cannot identify with that kind of Christ in a racist society. . . . [The] sin of Evangelicalism is not that we are un-American. It is rather that we are more American than Christian.[11]

The most prominent and outspoken critic of Evangelical racism is, of course, Black Evangelist Tom Skinner—who, incidentally, was vice-chairman of the Evangelicals for McGovern Committee. The son of a Baptist pastor, Skinner already hated whites at the age of fourteen. Twenty-two notches on his knife handle marked how many bodies he had slashed as leader of the Harlem Lords before his conversion to Christ in 1956, when a new Tom Skinner boldly walked out of that gang, untouched. Now he is a full-time evangelist and minister in the mainline National Baptist Convention, USA.

Skinner is the author of three books, *Black and Free*, his autobiography, *Words of Revolution*, and *How Black Is the Gospel?* (Phila. and N.Y.: Lippincott, 1970), in which he argues for "a gospel which is genuinely black, even as it is genuinely white: multicolored, universal, the only hope for a sinful world in desperate need of God's redeeming grace" (p. 125). But probably his most powerful statement on the necessity of a nonracist Christian message was Skinner's speech to the Young Evangelicals at Urbana '70, for which he received a standing ovation. In it, he blasts without apology the hypocrisy of Evangelical churches:

> To a great extent the evangelical church in America supported the status quo. It supported slavery; it supported segregation; it preached against any attempt of the black man to stand on his own two feet. And those who sought to communicate the gospel to black people did it in a way to make sure that they stayed cool. "We will preach the gospel to those folks so they won't riot; we will preach the gospel to them so that we can keep the lid on the garbage pail." And so they were careful to point out such scriptures as, "Obey your masters," "Love your enemy," "Do good to them that hurt you." But no one ever talked about a message which would also speak to the oppressor (*Christ the Liberator*, p. 194).

The Black evangelist also repudiates the god of the American civil religion and affirms the God of Jesus Christ who frees men and women from every kind of oppression and bondage:

> I as a black Christian have to renounce Americanism. I have to renounce any attempt to wed Jesus Christ to the American system. I disassociate myself from any argument that says a vote for America is a vote for God. I dissociate myself from any argument that says God is on our side. I disassociate myself from any argument which says that God sends troops to Asia, that God is a capitalist, that God is a militarist, that God is the worker behind our system.
>
> The thing you must recognize is that Jesus Christ is no more a capitalist than he is a socialist or a communist. . . . He is the Lord of heaven and earth. And if you are going to respond to Jesus Christ, you must respond to him as Lord (*Christ the Liberator*, pp. 204–205).

For Skinner, Jesus was a true radical who was crucified for his revolutionary activity. And as the risen Lord of the universe, he is now the model for and power behind a revolution the victory of which is sure. Christ invites all men and women to join that revolution by committing themselves to him, and then by proclaiming and demonstrating to the world that the Liberator has come to loose those who are bound spiritually, mentally, and physically:

Three days . . . [after his death] Jesus Christ pulled off one of the greatest political coups of all time: He got up out of the grave. When he arose from the dead, the Bible now calls him the second man, the new man, the leader of a new creation—a Christ who has overthrown the existing order and established a new order that is not built on man. . . .

You will never be radical until you become part of that new order and then go into a world that is enslaved. . . (*Christ the Liberator*, p. 208).

The Young Evangelicals are indeed responding to the call of Christ to enlist in his contemporary revolution—to challenge all unbiblical and unscientific racism in the churches and in society at large against Black people, Mexican and Puerto Rican Americans, Native Americans, Asian Americans, and all other disenfranchised minorities. These young men and women realize that to believe in a Lord who can liberate the soul but leaves the body enslaved is to believe in no liberator at all. The Young Evangelicals are convinced, however, that their Lord Jesus Christ does have the power to liberate the captives, to give sight to the blind, to set at liberty them that are bruised. And they go in his power, telling and demonstrating to the world by their lives that the Liberator has come.

4. The Politics of Conscience: The People's Christian Coalition and Senator Mark Hatfield

The world expects of Christians that they will raise their voices so loudly and clearly and so formulate their protest that not even the simplest man can have the slightest doubt about what they are saying. Further, the world expects of Christians that they will eschew all fuzzy abstractions and plant themselves squarely in front of the bloody face of history. We stand in need of folk who have determined to speak directly and unmistakably and come what may, to stand by what they have said.

Albert Camus

Blessed are the peacemakers, for they shall be called sons of God.

Matthew 5:9

In keeping with their traditional attachment to the political status quo, Evangelicals and Fundamentalists have generally sided with those who urge war as inevitable and with those who defend injustice in the name of law and order. This does not mean, of course, that a few notable exceptions do not appear in the course of recent history—persons like the brave Dutchwoman, Corrie Ten Boom, who with her family was incarcerated under the Nazis for harboring Jews and was the only one of that family to walk out of the concentration camp alive. In America, a good number—if not most—Fundamentalists and Establishment Evangelicals are also conservative Republicans (or the equivalent). Richard Pierard, an Evangelical and professor of history at Indiana State University, in his book, *The Unequal Yoke: Evangelical Christianity and Political Conservatism* (Phila. and N.Y.: Lippincott, 1970), traces the growing affinity between Christian Orthodoxy, political and economic conservatism, and American nationalism. He argues that this "unequal yoke" is, in fact, quote contrary to the Christian virtues of love for one's neighbor, selflessness, humility, and peacefulness (incidentally, Jesus did not bless the peace *lovers*, he blessed the peace*makers*). Pierard then goes on to declare that the unequal yoke must be broken if the Christian faith is to confront in a meaningful way the enormous sociopolitical problems of the next decade.

The Young Evangelicals readily accept Richard Pierard's argument and are manifestly discerning the need for committed Christians to join other men and women of good will in the arena of politics to work for righteous social change that only political action can bring about. They realize that it is one thing to "be subject to the governing authorities" (Romans 13:1) under a régime such as the Roman Empire in which constructive change seemed hopeless, but it is quite another to sit back and support an unjust political status quo in a relative democracy like the United States where change *is* possible by means of political and economic pressure and the democratic process.

The People's Christian Coalition in Deerfield, Illinois (founded in 1971), is a group of activist Young Evangelicals who espouse a theology of "Christian radicalism." Many of these young men and women were students at Trinity Evangelical Divinity School. The coalition publishes a sophisticated bimonthly underground newspaper, *The Post-American*, edited by Jim Wallis, which relates the mandates of biblical faith to the resolution of contemporary social and political issues. In a letter written to the author, Dennis MacDonald, an associate editor of *The Post-American*, says:

We see our main ministry as articulating a radical Christian response to war and injustice, and as organizing groups and individuals committed to this into a network for prophetic action in Amerika.

As far as we can tell, we are the most organized and aggressive group with this understanding of the gospel east of the Rockies, but we are not interested in a strong organization at all. Our hopes lie in the moral awakening of the evangelical community. . . .

Rather than functioning merely as a political pressure group, the People's Christian Coalition operates to encourage costly discipleship that inherently demands prophetic social and political action in our present turbulent society. The basic stance of this vocal organization of Young Evangelicals is reflected in its well-articulated statement of purpose printed in each issue of *The Post-American:*

We fault theological liberalism which neglects man's need of personal transformation and while holding to a pollyanna view of humanity, distorts the historic content of the Christian faith and retreats to ecclesiastical hierarchies. We fault a narrow orthodoxy that speaks of salvation but is often disobedient to the teachings of the prophets, the apostles, and Christ Himself, who clearly state that faith divorced from a radical commitment to social justice is a mockery. We dedicate ourselves to no ideology, government, or system, but to active obedience to our Lord and His Kingdom, and to sacrificial service to the people for whom He died.

Our faith must be distinctively Post-American, because of the offense of established religion the proclamation and practice of a caricature of Christianity so enculturated, domesticated, and lifeless that our generation easily rejects it as ethically insensitive, hypocritical, and irrelevant to the needs of our times. The church has lost its prophetic voice and has become the chaplain of the American nation preaching a harmless folk religion of convenience, conformity, and Presidential prayer breakfasts. . . .

Christian radicalism provides the vehicle for people willing to change their own lives, to challenge the system, to take the problem of change seriously. Christians must be active in rejecting the corrupt values of our culture, prophetic in our resistance and activism against the injustice of a racist society, welfare state, and exploitative system. The determination of the movemental church is to be those of a new order who live by the values and ethical priorities of Jesus Christ and His Kingdom in the midst of the indifference and injustice of the American church and state.

One of the contributing editors to *The Post-American* is Senator Mark Hatfield, whose Christian witness in political life has been well known for many years—during his tenure as a member of the House of Representatives, governor of Oregon, and now United States senator (re-elected in 1972 for a second term).

Hatfield, a Conservative Baptist layman, has received much criticism from other Evangelicals for his unreserved opposition to the use of American forces in Indochina, his liberal foreign and domestic policies in general, and his explicit rejection of the American civil religion. At the same time, however, probably most Evangelicals and even Open Fundamentalists respect the man for not hesitating to give a public account of his faith, whether or not they condone his legislative record. We have already mentioned in this regard that Billy Graham counseled Richard Nixon in 1968 to select Hatfield as his running mate.

The Republican senator's firm commitment to biblical faith is expressed vividly in his book, *Conflict and Conscience* (Waco, Texas: Word Books, 1972), a collection of speeches and writings Hatfield has produced over the last few years. Here he shows how his Orthodoxy actually impelled him to become one of his party's most outspoken liberals. Perhaps the best selection in Hatfield's book is his 1970 commencement address at Fuller Theological Seminary in which he argues for a necessary integration of personal evangelism and social action. Says the senator from Oregon:

Evangelicals have lost sight of the fact that the great issues being debated today are no longer those pertaining to organic evolution. Now they are those pertaining to social revolution.

We can no longer afford the supposed luxury of social withdrawal, but must find viable means to relate the Good News to the turmoil of our era. And as we have addressed ourselves to the theological problems of organic evolution in the past, let us turn to the theological problems of social revolution in the present. To do less is to concern ourselves with only half of the gospel.

Just because many theological liberals have upset the balance between dogma and ethics in one direction is no reason for us to upset it in another. Insofar as we preach only half the gospel, we are no less heretical than those who preach only the other half. It is my hope that evangelical Christianity will be led in a return to the entirety of the gospel (p. 25).

To declare that Orthodoxy, by neglecting the social dimension of the Gospel, is no less heretical than Liberalism is something that will not please Fundamentalists and Establishment Evangelicals who at best subordinate social action to traditional personal evangelism. But then Mark Hatfield has never been known to keep silent when his Christian conscience dictates otherwise. For instance, writing in the *Los Angeles Times*, he recently spoke out against the degradation, cheapening, and dehumanization of life in contemporary America, saying

Human life became cheap, and easily expendable—especially Asian life, which somehow seemed less valuable than American life. We justified policies by talking about body counts. And we destroyed all sensitivity to the sanctity of human life.

That is what happened in Attica. That is what happens whenever we heed the frightened and vengeful pleas for "law and order" that would have us crush the lives of others.

The same holds true for capital punishment. Those who clamor for capital punishment—even for those certain "exceptions"—do not sense how basic a right they would deny.

A sense that life comes cheap plagues our attitudes regarding amnesty. We would ostracize young men from our midst—ban them forever from our land —because we disagree with their conscience. It means we have little respect for their lives.[12]

One of the most significant actions taken recently by the senator from Oregon was his biblical condemnation of the American civil religion at the 1973 presidential prayer breakfast, an annual affair since 1953, which typically confuses religion with nationalism. Having been invited to speak by Senator John Stennis (D–Miss), chairman of that breakfast (just before he was shot), Hatfield warned his Democratic counterpart that he would speak his mind to those in attendance. Stennis assured him of complete freedom; thus the Republican senator indeed spoke to that gathering—which included the president, Billy Graham, and the mayor of Moscow—in a manner reminiscent of the Old Testament prophets:

My brothers and sisters, as we gather at this prayer breakfast, let us beware of the real danger of misplaced allegiance, if not outright idolatry, to the extent that we fail to distinguish between the god of an American civil religion and the God who reveals himself in the holy Scriptures and in Jesus Christ.

If we as leaders appeal to the god of civil religion, our faith is in a small and exclusive deity, a loyal spiritual adviser to power and prestige, a defender of only the American nation, the object of a national folk religion devoid of moral content. But if we pray to the biblical God of justice and righteousness, we fall under God's judgment for calling upon his name but failing to obey his commands. . . .

We sit here today as the wealthy and the powerful. But let us not forget that those who follow Christ will more often find themselves not with comfortable majorities, but with miserable minorities. Today our prayers must begin with repentance. Individually, we must seek forgiveness for the exile of love from our hearts. And corporately, as a people, we must turn in repentance from the sin that has scarred our national soul. "If my people . . . shall humble themselves, and pray, and seek my face, and turn from their wicked ways . . . then I will forgive their sins, and will heal their land" (II Chron. 7:14).

We need a "confessing church"—a body of people who confess Jesus as Lord and are prepared to live by their confession. Lives lived under the lordship of Jesus Christ at this point of our history may well put us at odds with values of our society, abuses of political power, and cultural conformity of our church. We need those who seek to honor the claims of their discipleship—those who live in active obedience to the call: "Do not be conformed to this world, but be transformed by the renewing of your minds" (Rom. 12:2). We must continually be transformed by Jesus Christ and take his commands seriously. Let us be Christ's messengers of reconciliation and peace, giving our lives over to the power of his love. Then we can soothe the wounds of war, and renew the face of the earth and all mankind.[13]

In the wake of the ever uglier political corruption evidenced by Watergate and related events, the continued pervasiveness of militarism in our national life, the manifest hypocrisy of civil religion, and the seeming lack of social compassion on the part of the present political establishment, the People's Christian Coalition and Senator Mark Hatfield both have given the Young Evangelicals new hope for the future and thus serve to strengthen their fresh priorities of national and world peace, and an active involvement in the politics of conscience.

5. & 6. The Fight Against Poverty and the Struggle for a Healthy Environment

I was hungry and you blamed it on the communists.
I was hungry and you circled the moon.
I was hungry and you told me to wait.
I was hungry and you set up a commission.
I was hungry and you said, "So were my ancestors."
I was hungry and you said, we don't hire over 35.
I was hungry and you said, God helps those . . .
I was hungry and you told me I shouldn't be.
I was hungry and you told me machines do that work now.
I was hungry and you had napalm bills to pay.
I was hungry and you said, the poor are always with us.
Lord, when did we see you hungry?

variation on Matthew 25:37,
in *The Post-American*

The Bible has a good deal to say about Heaven, but it has even more to say about the earth. The attitude of the sacred writers toward the earth was strangely affectionate. It is obvious that they loved it and appreciated its bounty. The very first book describes the Creator looking upon this planet with its fertile grass, its herbs and trees, and seeing that it was good. In the final book the angels are warned by the Great Judge not to hurt the earth, the grass, the trees, or the sea. The psalmist composes some of his most beautiful lyrics about the earth as a place overflowing with riches and goodness and love and praise. The earth is honored by the presence of Deity: "He visits the earth and waters it." The earth is filled with divine glory and blessed with life-giving powers. From the dust of the earth man was first formed. He was put on the earth to till and replenish it, and to sustain himself from its bountiful supply. The most beloved of all the psalms is a picture of domesticated animals, green pastures, and still waters—the earth.

Sherwood Eliot Wirt,
*The Social Conscience
of the Evangelical*

The fight against poverty and the struggle for a sound ecology go hand in hand. For the committed Christian, both efforts are aimed at realizing the "abundant life" Christ wills for all men and women. And both demand a measure of self-sacrifice. To correct poverty in America, there must be a more equitable distribution of wealth, which means, among other things, higher taxes—especially for the rich. On the world level, alleviation of poverty requires that the wealthy, developed nations give generously to the poorer, developing countries. That kind of action will also be a costly endeavor for Americans. Then, to correct flagrant abuses of the natural environment, self-sacrifice again is necessary. In fighting air pollution, many people will have to give up their luxury cars for smaller, less powerful, and less polluting makes. Others will have to relinquish their automobiles altogether in favor of public mass transit which itself must be supported, in part at least, by higher taxes. Preservation of the land, soil, natural vegetation, and wildlife demands increased and more effective governmental control in general together with additional state and national parks and wilderness areas in particular. Building will have to be restricted to ensure respect for the ecological balance, while more money must be spent on water purification, recycling of wastes, and finding alternative food and energy sources. The freedom of those who willfully pollute the environment will have to be abridged. In a word, the emerging struggle for a healthy natural environment *necessarily* means costly self-denial both on the part of individuals and society as a whole. Tragically, Evangelicals and Fundamentalists have again sided with the status quo on the issues of poverty and pollution and, in so doing, have sanctified the supposed virtue of selfishness.

The nineteen richest nations of the world represent only 16 percent of the total population, but these same nations control 75 percent of the world's income. Thus the vast majority of the people of the world are poor, hungry, subject to one disease after another, and live in conditions which can only be termed inhuman. Poverty exists in wealthy America as well, however, in Black ghettos and Chicano barrios, in inner cities and depressed rural areas, among Mexican-American farmworkers and the elderly who must rely on subsistence wages and welfare (or other fixed income) respectively. Why poverty in America? In treating the issue, Oscar Lewis suggests that poverty develops in many historical contexts, but, in particular, tends to *thrive* in societies manifesting the following conditions:

(1) a cash economy with labor and profit production, (2) a chronically high rate of unemployment or underemployment of unskilled laborers, (3) low wages, (4) a failure of the society to provide adequate social, political and economic organi-

zations, either through private or government agencies, for the poor, (5) the existence of a bilateral rather than unilateral kinship system and, finally, (6) the existence of a set of values in the dominant class which stresses the accumulation of wealth and property, emphasizes the possibility of upward mobility and thrift, and perceives low socioeconomic status as an outcome of personal inadequacy and/or inferiority.[14]

It is the last point that pertains especially to America and her devotion to the Protestant ethic. Evangelicals and Fundamentalists, in particular, uphold the notion that hard work, high production, and the success these are expected to bring are the cornerstone of our society. Poverty, they feel, is merely the result of refusal to work ("I fight poverty. I work."). But such an understanding of poverty ignores the inevitable lack of incentive among the poor. It neglects the reality that

accompanying the lack of adequate income are the probabilities of illness, inferior and incomplete educations, limited availability of information, inaccessabiity to resources, limited access to transportation and those other things which together provide the ability to move toward economic independence in our society. The fact that one's parents are poor almost invariably means that they cannot provide the means to better health and education which are necessary to improve one's worth in an industrial economy.[15]

Middle-class Orthodoxy in America often quotes the words of Jesus, "The poor you always have with you . . ." (John 12:8) to justify the existence of poverty. Yet, this usage of Scripture totally disregards context. Here Jesus was simply making an historical statement in an historical context, the point of which was his forthcoming crucifixion (hence, ". . . but you do not always have me."). As James Johnson, professor of history at Bethel College, St. Paul, Minnesota, maintains in *The Cross & The Flag:*

Let those who want to know what Christ taught about poverty read the four gospels, particularly Matthew 25:31–46. They will find that He moved regularly among the poor, instructed them, made Himself available to them, and in general lifted their spirits. At the same time He condemned the dishonest rich and challenged all wealthy people to be better men and not merely better off. Twentieth-century evangelical Christians who desire to be as faithful as possible to the teachings of Christ might well ask themselves, not how much the poor enter into the life of their churches, but how much their churches enter into the life of the poor (pp. 173–174).

We have already mentioned the fact that Fundamentalists and Evangelicals prefer to treat the symptoms of poverty with benevolence rather than to seek its cure with corporate political action. Orthodox churches in Protestantism are too often associated with the rich, the employer class, the local establishment, whatever that might be. For these churches, collecting old clothes and canned foods for the poor at Christmastime or operating a rescue mission on skid row is far less costly than working for reformist political candidates or legislative bills which would raise taxes.

Nevertheless, *some* mainstream Ecumenical Liberal churches and organizations have moved beyond the traditional paths of fighting poverty—hospitals, orphanages, and homes for the aged—into the ghettos themselves in an effort to supplement government aid. For instance, the American Lutheran Church recently invested $1,250,000 in programs to help minority groups. The United Presbyterian Church in the USA made one million dollars available for investment in New York City ghetto housing and businesses. The National Council of Churches has rallied to the defense of Community Action Programs sponsored by the now seemingly defunct Office of Economic Opportunity, while the Friends (Quakers) of Philadelphia initiated a program of self-help housing in which they aided in buying and improving old homes for families who would assist in the renovation. But the participation of Orthodoxy in practical programs of this kind has been minimal. Furthermore, Protestant churches in general are forsaking the inner city for what Tom Skinner calls "suburban bliss"—there to forget the problem of poverty altogether. And while Evangelical and Fundamentalist churches continue to increase their giving to foreign mission endeavors, they forget their mission responsibilities (in social action) at home.

At any rate, in an urbanized, technological society, it will never be sufficient for churches and individual Christians to fight poverty by themselves. To *cure* that pressing social ill, they will have to join together with other people of good will in the political arena where the mandate for social change can be translated into effective action.

With respect to the present struggle for a healthy natural environment, Fundamentalism and Evangelicalism (no less than Liberalism, really) have actually been a *cause* of the contemporary ecological crisis. Lynn White, Jr., professor of history at UCLA and a world authority on Medieval technology, insists that the problem is due to the orthodox

Christian (an inclusive designation here) arrogance toward nature. Calling for a drastic re-thinking of modern Christianity, White finds inspiration in the thought of St. Francis:

> The key to an understanding of Francis is his belief in the virtue of humility —not merely for the individual but for man as a species. Francis tried to depose man from his monarchy over creation and set up a democracy of all God's creatures. With him the ant is no longer simply a homily for the lazy, flames a sign of the thrust of the soul toward union with God; now they are Brother Ant and Sister Fire, praising the Creator in their own ways as Brother Man does in his. . . .
>
> The present increasing disruption of the global environment is the product of dynamic technology and science which were originating in the Western medieval world against which Saint Francis was rebelling in so original a way. Their growth cannot be understood historically apart from distinctive attitudes toward nature which are deeply grounded in Christian dogma. . . . No new set of basic values has been accepted in our society to displace those of Christianity. Hence we shall continue to have a worsening ecological crisis until we reject the Christian axiom that nature has no reason for existence save to serve man.
>
> The greatest spiritual revolutionary in Western history, Saint Francis, proposed what he thought was an alternative Christian view of nature and man's relation to it: he tried to substitute the idea of equality of all creatures, including man, for the idea of man's limitless rule of creation. He failed. Both our present science and our present technology are so tinctured with orthodox Christian arrogance toward nature that no solution for our ecologic crisis can be expected from them alone. Since the roots of our trouble are so largely religious, the remedy must also be essentially religious, whether we call it that or not. We must rethink and refeel our nature and destiny. The profoundly religious, but heretical, sense of the primitive Franciscans for the spiritual autonomy of all parts of nature may point a direction. I propose Francis as a patron saint for ecologists.[16]

Indeed, it is not the Church which has called attention to the wholesale exploitation of our natural environment, but rather purely humanistic organizations like the Sierra Club, and more recently, Friends of the Earth. Despite the reality of God's revelation of himself in nature—a fact not emphasized in Orthodoxy—Christians and their religious institutions have preferred again to side with the status quo in a laissez-faire attitude which is more interested in so-called progress (i.e., better business and technological advance) and making money than in protecting the environment God has entrusted to all of us. In the words of Earl Reeves, an Evangelical and professor of political science at the University of Tulsa:

The Christian's God is infinite, but the world He has entrusted to His created beings is not. The scriptural warning, "Whatsoever a man sows, that he will also reap" (Gal. 6:7), must not be ignored. If man continues the present pattern of senseless exploitation, then he will reap the destruction of the earth whose care has been entrusted to him. . . . Ecology has become a cause. But it is a cause that may well flounder in futility unless the Christian . . . can help establish a set of values that places life and its support system ahead of convenience and supposed economic need (*The Cross & The Flag*, pp. 200–201).

Like other young men and women in America today, the Young Evangelicals have expressed their concern for the alleviation of poverty and the realization of a healthier natural environment by concrete action with little or no pay—in the ghettos, in depressed rural areas, among the farmworkers and others alienated from the mainstream of American society, and as active members of organizations dedicated to the cause of ecology. Thus, they have taken seriously Christ's invitation to life— and a more abundant life at that.

7. In, Not of the World

> . . . for the LORD sees not as man sees; man looks on the outward appearance, but the LORD looks on the heart.
>
> I Samuel 16:7

> . . . I came that they may have life, and have it abundantly.
>
> John 10:10

> The Church as a body has never made up her mind about the arts, and it is hardly too much to say that she has never tried. She has, of course, from time to time puritanically denounced the arts as irreligious and mischievous, or tried to exploit the arts as a means to the teaching of religion and morals—but . . . both these attitudes are false and degrading.
>
> Dorothy Sayers

Apart from identifying closely with the civil religion, American Orthodoxy has still not made its peace with culture, and so continues to espouse an almost entirely negative personal ethic of "don'ts." Often implicit within Evangelicalism and Fundamentalism is the feeling associated with Puritanism that anything fun is necessarily evil—"illegal, immoral or fattening." Also, we have already mentioned the gnostic influence on Orthodox Christianity—its inherent belief that only the spirit ought to be cultivated, since the flesh (especially sex) is altogether bad. Then, as John Warwick Montgomery, professor of church history at Trinity Evangelical Divinity School, states: "the condemnation of old evils (card-playing, dancing, the theater, tobacco, liquor—all associated with the wide-open frontier towns) became a liturgy to be repeated by outspokenly nonliturgical believers, regardless of the social evils currently in vogue, and in spite of widely changing mores."[17] In other words, the "cultural baggage" of revivalism (including taboos against those old evils) have become articles of doctrine and tests of fellowship within contemporary Orthodoxy as a whole. But this baggage—notions, theories, expectations, and practices—belonged properly to a specific historical, sociocultural context (i.e., late nineteenth and early twentieth-century revivalism) where it had its own validity. And cultural baggage which has validity in one cultural context does not have the same validity in another. Baggage is culturally (not biblically) determined; thus it is nontransferable. In fact, outmoded, culturally determined taboos and expectations (e.g., having to do with hair length, style of dress, acceptable music, art and recreation) lacking biblical justification conflict with and retard desirable development, progress, and freedom in the present.

Why, we may well ask, does Orthodox Christianity generally ban *certain* kinds of cultural participation apart from a solid biblical prohibition against these activities? Quite often, Fundamentalists and Evangelicals *first* decide that something is wrong, *then* go to the Bible to "dig up" scriptural justification. This, of course, leads to bad exegesis, removal of passages from their proper context, and the use of arguments which are simply *one* possible and legitimate interpretation of complex biblical materials (another could just as easily have been brought forward). Once "proof texts" are discovered, a supposed scriptural prohibition becomes doctrine, and no other way is then allowed. For example, taboos characteristically held by Orthodoxy which are culturally rather than biblically determined are applied against (1) drinking, (2) smoking, (3) card-playing and gambling, (4) social dancing, (5) rock music, (6) long hair on men, and (7) attendance at the theater.

First, it is felt that drinking leads *inevitably* to alcoholism, sex, and crime. But does it, in fact? Although the Bible is clear in its condemnation of drunkenness, a biblical case can be made *either* for abstinence or moderation, as even Sherwood Wirt, editor of the Billy Graham Evangelistic Association's *Decision* magazine admits. Jesus himself was happy to provide wine—and very good wine in quantity—for the marriage feast at Cana (John 2:1–12). Would he have done so if drinking were inherently evil? If Evangelicalism and Fundamentalism in the United States usually prohibit even the moderate use of alcohol, such is not the case in various other countries (especially those in Continental Europe). And it was only after 1815 that abstinence took precedence over moderation in American Christianity, according to Paul Ramsey, professor of Christian ethics at Princeton University.

Second, smoking (and the use of tobacco in general) is condemned largely because it was once associated with the town pool hall and persons who regularly engaged in promiscuous or just "nasty" behavior —criminal types in the city and those who frequented the wild frontier towns. It was an "appearance of evil" (I Thess. 5:22 KJV). Increasingly, however, Fundamentalists and Evangelicals are realizing that tobacco use is no longer associated *only* with unrighteous people and cultural settings; so, they are beginning to adopt the more legitimate argument that smoking is unhealthy and thus should be avoided. But no distinction is made between cigarette-smoking and the use of cigars, a pipe, chewing tobacco, or snuff.

Third, card-playing is frowned upon because it necessarily meant gambling in the wide-open frontier towns. Such may also be the case in Las Vegas and Reno today. But why should card-playing as an enjoyable form of recreation be banned altogether for this reason alone? (Incidentally, gambling itself is considered a vice chiefly within the Anglo-Saxon tradition. Roman Catholics and Lutherans, for instance, have never thought it to be wrong.)

Fourth, social dancing is prohibited because it is thought *inevitably* to lead to illicit sexual activity. But does it? In their positive discussion of rock music, *Rock, Bach & Superschlock* (Phila. and N.Y.: A.J. Holman, 1972), Harold Myra and Dean Merrill (both of the Youth for Christ staff) argue that social dancing is not evil per se. Rather, the two Young Evangelicals contend, it is bad actions of some dancers that constitute evil. Writing specifically for teenagers, they say:

Granted, some American teen-agers use rock rhythms for some pretty sexy dancing, the kind of thing that belongs only in a married couple's bedroom. But what a copout to say, "The rhythm made me do it!" What about the floor, and the kids' shoes, and the Cheerios that gave them the energy? Are they also to blame? No way . . . the dancer himself is fully responsible for what he communicates through his motions. The music only makes things convenient for what he wants to express anyway.

Rock rhythms are used every day as, among other things, a simple expression of happiness by thousands of American teen-agers (p. 55).

Fifth, rock music in general is felt to be evil (some say demonic), because its lyrics are "filthy" and (again) its rhythms erotic. Here Harold Myra and Dean Merrill remind us that those who *want* to find filth in rock lyrics may be successful. In some, but certainly not all songs depravity is suggested. But really, is it not merely a matter for the listener to sort the good from the bad and dwell on the former (in the same way a dancer can avoid certain gestures)? Just as we cannot insulate ourselves from every speck of dirt in literature and art, so we must accept some bad with the good in music. And clearly, there is no reason why rock music itself cannot function as a legitimate expression of happiness for Christian young people.

Since the advent of the Jesus People, Gospel-rock has made its way into the life of numerous Evangelical churches, but usually only if the rhythm is toned down and the lyrics are Christianized. Myra and Merrill welcome the emergence of Gospel-rock; at the same time, these Young Evangelicals argue that music in general and rock in particular need not be religious to be good and even instructive, because "when you write about God and His creation—you've included everything!" (p. 56):

Truth sometimes pops up in odd places. During World War II, the Nazis had a slight problem of what to do about the obviously superb classical music written by Jews—Mendelssohn, for example. It was downright painful for them to have to recognize excellence from that kind of source! So they had the music printed with only the word "Anonymous" at the top of the page, or else they banned it altogether.

Well, a man doesn't have to be a Nazi to write quality music or do other outstanding things. Nor does he have to be a Christian. A surgeon may be a wife-beater or a drunk—and still be able to save your life. A professor may have twisted ideas about God, but know a great deal about calculus. A rock group may be fairly crude and indecent, and yet quite articulate in describing alienation or loneliness.

The Christian doesn't need to let this bother him. People are simply smart in some areas and stupid in others, that's all. We can benefit from brilliance wherever we find it, while ignoring spots where the same people don't know what they're talking about (p. 119).

Sixth, long hair on men has recently become a special taboo within Orthodoxy, allegedly because of I Corinthians 11:14: "Does not nature itself teach you that for a man to wear long hair is degrading to him?" But it appears in this verse that Paul (as he does elsewhere) is speaking to his own time and culture. What happens when long hair becomes the normal style for men in a given society? Furthermore, this taboo among Evangelicals and Fundamentalists has probably more to do with the aversion of Middle America to long hair on men (i.e., it is not "masculine") than any biblical prohibition.

Seventh, Orthodox Christianity has traditionally looked down upon the theater and other forms of art because, as Dorothy Sayers puts it, they are "irreligious and mischievous." Fundamentalists and Evangelicals often fail to see that secular plays and films can, in fact, illumine the mind by depicting graphically important aspects of the human condition (that in addition to genuine entertainment). Moreover, while Orthodoxy still associates the theater with the baser elements of society and the "sinful" show business industry, it sees no reason why Christians cannot watch equivalent movies or plays on television.

Thus, we should now be able to discern the degree to which culture (rather than sound biblical exegesis) has affected the taboos and expectations of Orthodoxy in America. The Young Evangelicals insist that many forms of cultural participation may indeed be legitimate for Christians—e.g., moderate drinking, card-playing, social dancing, listening to rock music, and attendance at the theater—despite the fact that these have been traditionally banned by the majority of Evangelicals and Fundamentalists. In fact, they feel that such activities *can* be understood as God's good gifts for the use (not misuse) of his children. Freedom in Christ challenges the committed Christian to develop a sense of ethical *responsibility* rather than a legalism which is contrary to the spirit of the New Testament. At any rate, one thing is sure: the Young Evangelicals repudiate unreservedly the notion that external behavior and participation in contemporary culture should be the criteria by which the body of believers judges a man or woman's spirituality, for "man looks on the outward appearance, but the LORD looks on the heart."

D. THE MISSION OF THE CHURCH

It should now be manifestly apparent what the Young Evangelicals hope for the institutional church as it seeks to fulfill its mission in the world. First, these young men and women feel that the Church must always derive its authority for faith and action from the Bible—rightly understood as the Word of God written. Second, they recognize the absolute necessity of personal commitment to Jesus Christ as Savior and Lord, the results of which are complete life-transformation and a new beginning for the convert. Third, the Young Evangelicals believe in the mandate for evangelism—the proclamation and demonstration of the whole Gospel, relevant to every dimension of human life. Fourth, these young men and women sincerely hope that the institutional church will take the call to discipleship seriously by encouraging and teaching its membership to bear the cross, and by motivating each disciple of Christ to discover his or her Christian vocation following the principles outlined by Paul in Romans 12 and I Corinthians 12. They trust that the membership of the institutional church—in uncovering the deep meaning of discipleship—will join them, individually and corporately, in their fresh priorities which include (as we have seen) sexual love as a joyful experience, meaningful interpersonal and social relationships and the dignity of women, racial justice, peace and conscientious political involvement, the fight against poverty, a healthy natural environment, and a positive and happy participation in contemporary culture. Finally, the Young Evangelicals realize that renewal of the Church of Jesus Christ demands not only costly discipleship, but reconciliation, and Christian unity as well.

We have already ascertained that some of these young men and women (e.g., CWLF and the People's Christian Coalition) have found it expedient to forsake the institutional church—for the time being, anyway—in order to exercise their prophetic function without undue hindrance or restriction. They wish to influence the community of faith from outside institutional walls. Because we live in an era of seemingly healthy religious movements per se, there is no reason why the Young Evangelicals operating outside the institutional church cannot achieve some measure of success in attaining their goals. For, we must admit the contemporary viability of the persistence of a movement without coherent internal structure, hierarchy, or real membership—the existence in modern society of a looser affiliation, carried by the mass media, without the explicit need to bring people together for formal (as distinct from "expressive") purposes.

At the same time, as we have said, it is also true that numerous Young Evangelicals are trying hard to pursue renewal by remaining *within* the institutional church, both in the characteristically Evangelical structures and in the mainstream Ecumenical Liberal denominations (not to mention the Roman Catholic Church). Those who find themselves within the Liberal ecclesiastical institutions will advocate that their churches again take seriously the need for personal conversion to Christ and the desirability of a solid biblical-theological foundation for social action. On the other hand, those who stay within the Evangelical churches will probably be working to help translate biblical faith into Christian unity and concrete social involvement—conversion into discipleship. Thus, the Young Evangelicals can effectively promote renewal within the Evangelical structures no less than the mainstream Ecumenical Liberal denominations, and even outside the institutional church altogether.

Nevertheless, we should not neglect the fact that now (as perhaps never before) the opportunity for meaningful reconciliation between Christians of seemingly contrary ideologies is a distinct possibility. Reconciling the cleavage between Liberals and Evangelicals, therefore, ought to become a priority for both camps engaged in the present theological warfare. And it is also clear that the Young Evangelicals can play a significant role in this search for healing and real Christian unity. So we shall now seek to discover just how and through whom reconciliation might be effected and in what manner wholeness can be restored to the Body of Christ in America today.

VI. Toward a More Effective Ecumenism

Behold, how good and pleasant it is when brothers dwell in unity!

Psalms 133:1

. . . that they may all be one; even as thou, Father, art in me, and I in thee, that they also may be in us, so that the world may believe that thou hast sent me.

John 17:21

There is one body and one Spirit, just as you were called to the one hope that belongs to your call, one Lord, one faith, one baptism, one God and Father of us all, who is above all and through all and in all.

Ephesians 4:4–6

Evangelicals are not the only Christians. There are those who share with us a firm belief in historic, supernatural Christianity, who worship Christ as Lord and Savior, who take a high view of Scripture, yet who may not use all our terminology and who hold a view of the church and the ministry different from ours. They too are Christians; and from some of them we have much to learn.

Frank E. Gaebelein, Co-editor of
Christianity Today (1963–66)

. . . Consider a haunting question stated recently by several conservative evangelicals. They said, "We know there are many true evangelicals in the World Council of Churches. There are more in the World Council circles than outside. We have to ask, therefore, why they have accomplished so little." When one sees the futility of our churches in the face of so many problems of our time, one finds no easy answer to their question. Perhaps the first requisite for fellowship with Christians who criticize us so deeply is not self-defense, but repentance that our witness is so limited. It may be that in such shared repentance we will find that *given* unity in which the truth of Christ is fully manifest, and whereby the world may be led to saving faith.

Eugene L. Smith, former WCC
executive, *Christianity
Today* (1963)

When men are animated by the charity of Christ they feel united —and the needs, sufferings and joys of others are felt as their own.

Pope John XXIII

Almost always the creative dedicated minority has made the world better.

Martin Luther King, Jr.

We have said that the real Ecumenical problem in America today is not the existence side by side of a multitude of Protestant denominations. Nor is it simply Protestantism versus Catholicism. Rather, the critical Ecumenical issue now is the ever more visible cleavage between mainstream Ecumenical Liberalism and Evangelicalism. Thus, the question we must raise is whether some kind of meaningful reconciliation of this cleavage is possible or even desirable.

For both Evangelicals and Liberals, remaining divided would clearly be the easier course; division leaves the *pride* of both schools of thought intact. And the consequences of an unreconciled cleavage are beginning to become apparent. Evangelicalism is doing very well numerically and financially, and it gives every indication of further growth and success along its separate path, while Liberalism seems to be slowly dying. Before long, in fact, it may be more appropriate to speak of mainstream Evangelicalism rather than mainstream Ecumenical Liberalism. Nevertheless, although the *influence* of Liberalism within the Church universal will probably continue to decline under present circumstances, Liberal control of the historic denominations and the Ecumenical structures most likely will remain solid. The fact of the matter, however, is that the climate for reconciliation may be more favorable now than ever before, because, ironically, Liberals and Evangelicals are closer to each other today than either camp realizes. Fundamentalism, of course, can be expected to hold firm to its separatist stance. And radically secular Christianity will not generally cooperate with Orthodoxy in any form. But there are good reasons to believe that the Evangelical–Ecumenical cleavage *can* indeed be reconciled.

First of all, Evangelicals no longer are set on capturing the historic denominations and the Ecumenical structures from the Liberals. Given their own mounting strength and influence in general outside and even within the historic denominations, Evangelicals (including Neo-Pentecostals) do not consider such action a priority. Hence, in one sense, Liberalism need no longer be defensive. Nevertheless, it is also true that any meaningful reconciliation will require the willingness of Liberals to include proportionate representation of the Evangelical stance in circles of decision-making power *within* the mainstream ecclesiastical institutions. And for the first time, Evangelicals can dialogue and negotiate with Liberals from a position of strength, a fact which should without question increase their interest in a rapprochement.

Second, Liberals in their present decline are beginning to wonder whether the Evangelicals, in fact, have something important to offer men and women today that Liberalism itself cannot provide. Thus, Liberals are beginning to feel that they might be able to *learn* and *benefit* from a positive encounter with the Evangelical movement.

Third, as time passes and new generations arise, the bitterness characteristic of the Fundamentalist–Modernist Controversy and its aftermath will continue to diminish. For the Young Evangelicals, that debate is history—and the kind of history in which they cannot take pride. With the disappearance of bitterness, reconciliation becomes a more viable option.

A fourth good reason for hope, as we have seen, is the increasing convergence of values and priorities held by Evangelicals (the emerging generation, at least) and those espoused in principle by mainstream Ecumenical Liberals. This convergence can be illustrated by comparing the priorities and values of the Young Evangelicals with the goals established already in 1948 by the founding Amsterdam Assembly of the World Council of Churches:

Our coming together to form a World Council will be in vain unless Christians and Christian congregations everywhere commit themselves to the Lord of the Church in a new effort to seek together, where they live, to be His witnesses and servants among their neighbors. We have to remind ourselves and all men that God has put down the mighty from their seats and exalted the humble and meek. We have to learn afresh together to speak boldly in Christ's name both to those in power and to the people, to oppose terror, cruelty and race discrimination, to stand by the outcast, the prisoner and refugee. We have to make of the Church in every place a voice for those who have no voice, and a home where every man will be at home. We have to learn afresh together what is the duty of the Christian man or woman in industry, in agriculture, in politics, in the professions and in the home. We have to ask God to teach us together to say No and to say Yes in truth. No, to all that flouts the love of Christ, to every system, every program, and every person that treats any man as though he were an irresponsible thing or a means of profit, to the defenders of injustice in the name of order, to those who sow the seeds of war or urge war as inevitable; Yes, to all that conforms to the love of Christ, to all who seek for justice, to the peacemakers, to all who hope, fight and suffer for the cause of man, to all who —even without knowing it—look for new heavens and a new earth wherein dwelleth righteousness.[1]

Finally, there is evidence that Liberals and Evangelicals in general are becoming visibly uncomfortable treading their separate paths. Evangelicals are beginning to realize that their attempts at purely spiritual unity among themselves alone have been largely unsuccessful. Likewise, Liberals are finding it easier to understand that an Ecumenical movement which consciously excludes so great a segment of the contemporary Church as represented by the Evangelicals is not genuinely Ecumenical at all.

But in our discussion of reconciling the Ecumenical–Evangelical cleavage, we must take note of two important points before pursuing the matter any further. First, given the current disenchantment with building larger and more powerful institutions—reflecting the present desire to destructure society—Liberalism's once seemingly viable search for an institutional "super church" appears to be dead. Thus, whatever more fully united Church finally emerges will probably find its unity largely (but not entirely) in a noninstitutional form. Real spiritual unity, however, as manifested by the Charismatic movement, for instance, should not be dismissed either as an unrealistic or an undesirable goal. Such unity is good in itself, and it might also function as a healthy force for the renewal of *existing* ecclesiastical structures. Secondly, if a future rapprochement between Evangelicals and Liberals is indeed attempted, reconciliation can hardly come about unless the deep *theological* differences between the two camps are dealt with seriously, and unless mainstream Ecumenical Liberalism recognizes the significance Evangelicals will always attach to the inspiration and authority of Scripture, the necessity of personal commitment to Christ as Savior and Lord, and the mandate for evangelism.

The openness of the Young Evangelicals (not to mention the Ecumenical interest of the Charismatic movement) is a solid indication that reconciliation may be within reach. For although these irenic men and women do not now constitute vast numbers, they nonetheless represent no less than a creative and dedicated minority, many of whom will one day assume leadership and eventually command the support of the majority. If, in the case of most Christians, selfishness is the barrier to discipleship, pride is the impediment to unity.

A. SOME PRACTICAL SUGGESTIONS

Dialogue between Liberals and Evangelicals will, of course, continue to be useful. But dialogue can go only so far before its limitations become manifestly apparent. Good intentions expressed by kind words must always be followed by concrete actions lest hypocrisy raise its head. Hence, we shall now consider some practical steps that Evangelicals and mainstream Ecumenical Liberals might take respectively and without further delay for the sake of reconciliation.

1. Subversives for Christ

As future leaders of a fast-growing and seemingly healthy Evangelical movement, the Young Evangelicals are themselves now in a good position to help reconcile the Ecumenical–Evangelical cleavage. Given their fresh spirit of openness, these young and women should ponder at least three avenues toward reconciliation clearly open to them.

First, in deciding *who* they are and exactly *what* their mission in the world is going to be—in raising their consciousness—the Young Evangelicals must also determine what their relationship with mainstream Ecumenical Liberalism is going to be. The positive action of these young men and women now will most likely decide the Evangelical posture as a whole in years to come. Unquestionably, they could benefit in this connection from some corporate yet nonbureaucratic expression of unity among themselves for the sake of effectiveness. Perhaps it will soon be possible to talk about a Young Evangelical movement—unified by the biblically founded values and priorities already manifested within the various groups now in existence. But even apart from this kind of movemental unity, the Young Evangelicals at the present time as individuals and organizations can increase their contact with the Ecumenical movement in practical ways. For instance, members of campus groups like IVCF and some of the more progressive Jesus People could become acquainted with the various denominational and Ecumenical campus ministries serving their own college or university. Sincere personal encounter might lead, eventually, to cooperative action. Also, Young Evangelical pastors, directors of Christian education, and youth ministers could take part actively in local ministerial councils and councils of churches. Too often Evangelicals participate only in their own interchurch organizations. But if the values and priorities of the Young Evangelicals and mainstream Ecumenical Liberals *really* are similar, continued separation serves no concrete purpose. Since the feeling of rejection tends to be a chief cause of the separatist stance, these young men and women of Evangelical persuasion might become an instrument of healing merely by accepting their Ecumenical counterparts, by saying words to the effect that "We accept you as brothers and sisters in Christ. Let's pool the gifts our Lord has given us for a more effective witness." The Young Evangelicals thus might find a welcome in Ecumenical circles they never dreamed possible, for Liberals themselves cannot help being attracted to the dedication and strong biblical-theological foundation for action manifested by these young men and women. As Mark Hatfield has said, those who engage only in the social dimension of the Gospel are no more heretical than those who seek only the salvation of souls. Thus, Evangelicals who come to Christians presently alienated from them in a spirit of humility and love do so as beggars telling other beggars where to find bread. And believers, no less than unbelievers, need the continual nourishment of the bread of life that Christian fellowship provides.

Second, if the Young Evangelicals are truly bent on the renewal of their own churches, whether Evangelical or Liberal, they should strive diligently for positions of leadership in those churches. Knowing that Orthodoxy especially has high regard for its leaders, these young men and women ought to make every effort to serve on the various boards and committees and in the Christian education program of their churches. Particularly in Evangelicalism, Christian education is still an important aspect of the church's life—a very good place (i.e., in the Sunday school room) to raise the *right* questions and introduce the concrete demands of discipleship so often neglected at all levels of the Sunday school. By taking on positions of leadership in their churches, the Young Evangelicals will be able to influence positively their older and more conservative kindred. This is not to say, however, that such a path is inherently easy. The prophet often finds the least enthusiastic reception among his own people. On occasion, he may have to become a stranger in his own church—a "subversive" for Christ. But the Young Evangelical leader can be sure that if he remains faithful to the Word of God in all he says and does, it will not return to him empty. His advocacy of costly grace and outreaching fellowship with all those who love Jesus Christ may not be welcomed—whether his church is avowedly Liberal or Evangelical—but it may *uncover* the sins of selfishness and pride unrecognized by the membership and thus signal the beginning of change. In many churches, the first step toward meaningful reconciliation with Christians of other persuasions and denominational or theological labels will be taken when committed and *brave* leadership in those churches says authoritatively that it is right and provides concrete methods by which that reconciliation, at various levels, can be effected. The Young Evangelicals can provide that prophetic leadership. They should make every effort to become leaders, at least within their own tradition.

Finally, in striving for positions of leadership in their churches, the

Young Evangelicals should look beyond the local congregation to the denomination and interdenominational structures as well, again, whether such are Evangelical or Liberal. It is true that the mainstream Ecumenical Liberal denominational hierarchies and the Ecumenical structures appear to have consciously excluded Evangelicals from positions of decision-making power; but it is also true that Evangelicals themselves, often concerned only with "spiritual" matters, have traditionally shied away from ecclesiastical politics. At the same time, they have been the first to complain when the Evangelical position is not adequately represented within the councils of the Church. The hard fact of the matter is that the Church, like any other social institution, is political, and it therefore requires competent and dedicated politicians to bring about needed change. If the leaders of the old (though still not dead) World Student Christian Federation became the leaders of their own denominations and, more frequently, the World Council of Churches and its regional affiliates after they were founded, there is no reason why the leaders of today's strong and healthy Evangelical campus movements (such as IVCF, for instance) cannot emerge tomorrow as the leadership of whatever more fully united and renewed Church finally comes into being. In this connection, it would be good if some of the Young Evangelicals would see ecclesiastical politics as their calling.

One of the barriers to a meaningful Evangelical–Ecumenical rapprochement is that Evangelicals are still often wrongly branded by Liberals as obscurantist and anti-intellectual, despite their degrees and scholarly production. The problem is that most Evangelicals—or at least many of them—take their first professional degree in theology at an Evangelical seminary. Liberals still tend to view Evangelical divinity schools as academically unsophisticated havens of rest where current questions and issues are dodged in favor of devotion and piety. The Young Evangelicals know that is not the case; but those who decide on ecclesiastical politics as a career—who plan a seminary education— might well consider the mainstream Ecumenical Liberal schools of theology that historically have produced the best politicians. In America, those seminaries are also the most "prestigious"—Harvard Divinity School, Yale Divinity School, Union Theological Seminary (New York), and the University of Chicago Divinity School—and God knows that the Evangelicals could use a little prestige and status in the eyes of their

Liberal counterparts. Ironically perhaps, the Young Evangelicals who do apply to 'the big four' schools of theology may find their applications welcomed. For one thing, admissions committees at these seminaries are frequently impressed by the solid Christian commitment and clear calling of Evangelical applicants. In addition, Liberal faculty members of such divinity schools often feel an obligation to "enlighten" conservative ministerial hopefuls who will often return to their conservative traditions and do likewise.

But apart from any benefit Evangelicals themselves might receive from attending one of the big four seminaries, their presence itself could be a reconciling influence, and therefore, a good thing. Why, we might well ask? Mainstream Ecumenical Liberals need to learn firsthand that Evangelicals *are* capable of self-criticism and are also *genuine human beings* committed to discipleship and Christian unity *too!* By being good students at the Ecumenical schools, and by taking an active part in seminary projects and functions—from social action to parties— Evangelicals can actually be a *witness* to their faith. The stereotyped image of an Evangelical in the minds of Liberal professors and theological students (not a few of whom are ex-Evangelicals) is bad—often very bad—but the Young Evangelicals can change that image dramatically. Once the prospective ecclesiastical politician gains acceptance among his instructors and fellow-theologs, he may find himself able to advance the Evangelical cause even while still a student. For instance, Liberal seminaries are taking student power seriously. Thus, increased numbers of Evangelical students within their ranks (some of whom might even function on faculty selection committees) might constitute a better case for the hiring of Evangelical faculty members.

Of course, we have to recognize that three years or more at a mainstream Ecumenical Liberal divinity school for a Young Evangelical will not be easy. In such an institution, theology is not always a distinctively Christian enterprise; and the Evangelical student's faith will not only be challenged, it will be tried by fire. Nevertheless, to use an oft-quoted dictum, "The finest steel goes through the hottest fire." And surely faith that cannot be defended (and enriched) in the course of higher education *may* need to be reconstructed. Self-criticism demands nothing less.

The Young Evangelical who is also a graduate of Chicago, Union, Yale, or Harvard, will most likely find numerous Ecumenical doors open to him—doors that may well lead ultimately to positions of decision-making power within the historic (and even Evangelical) ecclesiastical structures. This is not to say that all Young Evangelicals (or even most of them) ought to forsake the Evangelical seminaries. For the latter institutions provide possibly the best practical education available for contemporary parish-related ministry—together with an environment which builds up rather than tears down Christian faith. But the ecclesiastical politician is a special kind of minister whose vocation is certain to be enhanced by a special kind of theological education—which the big four offer.

If the Young Evangelicals take these three avenues toward reconciliation seriously—sincere and increased Ecumenical contact on campus and elsewhere, dedicated and outspoken (if not subversive) leadership in the home church, and the call to ecclesiastical politics—they will soon find themselves liberated from the hypocritical Evangelical ghetto with its complacency and protective shelter. Thus, the Young Evangelicals can do their fair share in restoring wholeness to the Gospel. Obviously, such a course will take time. It means that these young men and women will have to repudiate the "instantism" characteristic of their generation as a whole. But then, patience is something the Holy Spirit might teach us all.

2. More Practical Suggestions

In general, the kinds of steps Liberals might take to reconcile the Evangelical–Ecumenical cleavage are not much different from those we have suggested for Evangelicals—particularly the Young Evangelicals.

First of all, since ignorance and misunderstanding of the "other side" —its self-identity and aspirations—is a major cause of division, Liberals should be encouraged to become *acquainted* with Evangelicals wherever they find themselves. This can be accomplished by (1) reading their literature (e.g., books published by InterVarsity Press, Eerdmans, Word, Creation House, Logos International, and Zondervan, and magazines like *HIS*, *Christianity Today*, and *Eternity*); (2) visiting their churches, conferences, and other gatherings; and most important, (3) seeking them out *personally* in a spirit of acceptance, humility, openness, and love. Pastors of larger churches might try to find willing Evangelicals to fill positions on their staffs. Too many Liberals are still living at the height of the Fundamentalist–Modernist controversy and might well be surprised how dramatically large segments of Orthodoxy have changed.

Second, mainstream Ecumenical Liberals must adopt a more positive way of thinking about their Evangelical kindred in Christ. They will have to repudiate the notion common within their ranks that the only heresy is Orthodoxy, that it is somehow impossible to be a contemporary and progressive Christian and *still* believe in the inspiration and authority of Scripture, the necessity of conversion, and the mandate for evangelism. As we have seen, modern man may not be so thoroughly secular as Liberals have hitherto supposed; therefore, the historic doctrines of the Church might, in fact, have significant relevance to the needs of humanity today.

Finally, the single most important course of action Liberals can take to reconcile the Ecumenical–Evangelical cleavage is to initiate a program of *affirmative action* to bring willing Evangelicals into positions of decision-making power within the ecclesiastical structures and institutions from which they are now virtually excluded: hierarchies of the historic denominations, the National Council of Churches, and the World Council of Churches; faculties of leading denominational and Ecumenical seminaries (not to mention college and university departments of religious studies); staff of the United Ministries in Higher Education; and the editorial boards of mainline religious periodicals. The speed at which this is done should match the urgency with which Blacks and other minorities, women and young people are now being brought into leadership in those structures. Representation *proportionate* with the numerical strength of Evangelicals within the mainstream Ecumenical Liberal denominations (not just tokenism) may be the *only* way to save those ecclesiastical institutions from a slow and painful decline and eventual death. And if Evangelicals are encouraged to take their places of leadership in the historic denominations and the Ecumenical Movement, those leaders will be able to translate Ecumenical concerns to their respective constituencies (they alone can do so). In addition, *if* Liberals begin taking Evangelicals seriously in the denominations and Ecumenical structures the former now control, it will become much more difficult for those Evangelicals now *outside* those institutions to justify their continued separation and general non-cooperation. Taxation without representation has led to the separatist stance (Liberals should realize this), so proportionate representation should lead to reconciliation.

Active Evangelical participation in the mainstream of Ecumenical life would not only encourage reconciliation between Liberals and Evangelicals; it would also bring to the faltering denominational and Ecumenical structures a new spiritual vitality and solid biblical-theological foundation from which to operate more forcefully and effectively in the contemporary world. And maybe, just maybe, the Ecumenical movement as a whole would at the same time regain some of its once-avid supporters, long disenchanted by what can only appear as its gradual decay into just another secular bureaucracy.

B. IN THE SPIRIT

We have now discussed some *practical* paths toward reconciliation both Evangelicals and Liberals can take. But there is also a *spiritual* dimension of Christian unity. For ultimately, it is the Holy Spirit himself who renews the Church and brings Christian believers together in a common fellowship—from an implicit to an explicit oneness. Evangelicals especially have too long insisted on *doctrinal* unity in truth (and where is it?) rather than *experiential* unity in the Truth—Jesus Christ himself. One group which seems to have found that dynamic experiential unity is Charismatic Renewal. We have suggested that the Young Evangelicals could profit from some corporate yet nonbureaucratic expression of unity for mutual support and "that the world may believe." In this connection, these young men and women might be able to learn something about unity from the Charismatic movement.

Despite its present or potential weaknesses admitted by Michael Harper himself—anti-intellectualism and unthinking Fundamentalism, pietism and social unconcern, and spiritual elitism—Charismatic Renewal, as we have seen, displays a remarkable kind of oneness among Christians of seemingly contrary theological and ecclesiastical persuasions. (Just as the Young Evangelicals are trying to rid themselves of the cultural baggage of revivalism, so, many Neo-Pentecostals are rejecting the cultural baggage of denominational or "Classical" Pentecostalism [e.g., characteristic speech patterns, prayer postures, mental processes, and expectations].) In the words of J. Rodman Williams, president of Melodyland Schools in Anaheim, California (a Columbia University-Union Theological Seminary Ph.D., and former professor of theology at Austin Presbyterian Theological Seminary in Texas, in *The Era of the Spirit* (Plainfield, N.J.: Logos International, 1971):

Again, this new world of the interpenetration of the spiritual and the natural not only brings into play spiritual powers but also enhances natural capacities and functions. By no means does the natural become less important, but it is given fuller power and direction under the impact of the Holy Spirit. The mind takes on keener awareness of the true shape of reality; the feelings become more sensitive to the moods, the concerns, the hopes of the world and of people; the will finds itself strengthened to execute with more faithfulness and determination those ethical actions to which it gives itself. Thus through the conjoining of the spiritual and the natural, in which strange powers penetrate and invigorate the natural realm (the vast area of the intellectual, the aesthetic, the moral), there is a renewal and advancement of the whole human situation.

Finally, this is a new world wherein there is the dawning of a profound and lasting unity among brethren. For in this movement of the Spirit what is implicit in the Christian community becomes explicit: not only the immediacy of God with man but also man with his neighbor. Here truly is the transcendence of ancient walls of creed and tradition, race and nationality, cultural, economic, and social differentiation by the overarching Spirit of love. Thus does the moving Spirit, interfusing and pervading all, bring about lasting unity in the bond of peace (p. 58).

Thus, Williams sees in the Charismatic movement today a new manifestation of spiritual power which does not provide a convenient "cop-out" from real life, but rather gives enhancement and meaning to everyday existence (natural capacities and functions), an immediacy not only of God with man but also man with his neighbor, and a profound and lasting unity among brethren. His concerns, then, appear to reflect the two major characteristics of Christian renewal today —discipleship and reconciliation. If the power of the Holy Spirit expressed in Neo-Pentecostalism is indeed great enough to bring deeply divided Christendom together *and* to motivate the life of discipleship, it can surely be termed a significant force for renewal in the contemporary Church. Or as Krister Stendahl, dean of the Harvard Divinity School, has said: "The 'flashlight church' does not have enough to offer. The high voltage religious experience is a breakthrough phenomenon because it is needed. If churches are not open to an infusion of high voltage, they are in real trouble. . . .

God is upping the voltage of the faith in many places. He knows that it could be dangerous but he knows that it is needed, and that is the new Pentecostalism."[2]

In conclusion, we are justified in our assertion that the Evangelical movement—particularly the Young Evangelicals (stressing discipleship) and Charismatic Renewal (emphasizing unity)—is one energetic attempt to maintain and renew the spirit of the New Testament and the primitive church in a secular (or unsecular) age.

Maybe the greatest sin of the Church is that she has consistently endeavored to put "God in the dock"—to *confine* the power of the Holy Spirit. Liberals try to restrict divine activity to the events of political history and to social ethics; Evangelicals to purely spiritual needs and theology; Pentecostals to supernatural intervention and the realm of personal experience. Dare we hope for an emerging Church which will be able to effectively integrate the ethical, theological, and experiential —the social compassion of Liberalism, the theological commitment of Evangelicalism, and the supernatural power witnessed and felt in Pentecostalism? Perhaps we can appropriately summarize by suggesting that reconciliation and discipleship are the marks of those who let God be God in obedience to his will and in a positive response to costly divine grace. For it is only in submission to God that we can find real liberation, as C. S. Lewis declares in a graphic account of his conversion:

You must picture me alone in that room at Magdalen [College, Oxford], night after night, feeling, whenever my mind lifted even for a second from my work, the steady, unrelenting approach of Him whom I so earnestly desired not to meet. That which I greatly feared had at last come upon me. In the Trinity Term of 1929 I gave in, and admitted that God was God, and knelt and prayed: perhaps, that night, the most dejected and reluctant convert in all England. I did not then see what is now the most shining and obvious thing; the Divine humility which will accept a convert even on such terms. The Prodigal Son at least walked home on his own feet. But who can duly adore that Love which will open the high gates to a prodigal who is brought in kicking, struggling, resentful, and darting his eyes in every direction for a chance to escape? The words *compelle intrare,* compel them to come in, have been so abused by wicked men that we shudder at them; but, properly understood, they plumb the depth of the Divine mercy. The hardness of God is kinder than the softness of men, and His compulsion is our liberation.[3]

The present revolution in Orthodoxy is nothing more and nothing less than a conviction borne out in practice that Jesus Christ is still in total command. And in that sense, it is merely the embodiment in action of that earliest creed of the Church—Jesus is Lord! *Hallelujah!*

Notes

I. Introduction: The Contemporary Evangelical Movement

1. For further discussion of the function of contemporary religion, see Thomas F. O'Dea, *The Sociology of Religion* (Englewood Cliffs, New Jersey: Prentice-Hall, 1966).

II. The New Evangelical Orthodoxy

1. Quoted in Louis Gaspar, *The Fundamentalist Movement* (The Hague and Paris: Mouton, 1963), p. 120.

2. Addison H. Leitch, *Winds of Doctrine* (Westwood, New Jersey: Revell, 1966), p. 62.

3. "Are You One in a Million?," *United Evangelical Action*, Spring 1973, p. 30.

4. Billy Graham, *World Aflame* (Garden City, New York: Doubleday, 1965), p. 181.

5. Lowell D. Streiker and Gerald S. Strober, *Religion and the New Majority: Billy Graham, Middle America, and the Politics of the 70s* (New York: Association Press, 1972), p. 190.

6. Graham, *World Aflame*, p. 187.

7. John C. Bennett, "Billy Graham in Oakland," *Christianity and Crisis*, October 4, 1971, pp. 195–197

8. Billy Graham, "A Clarification," *Christianity Today*, January 19, 1973, p. 416.

9. Frank E. Gaebelein, ed., "Why Christianity Today?" in *Christianity Today*, (Westwood, New Jersey: Spire Books, 1968), p. 13.

10. "Liberation" (editorial), *Christianity Today*, January 19, 1973, p. 407.

11. Donald G. Bloesch, "The New Evangelicalism," *Religion in Life*, Autumn 1972, p. 336.

12. Carl F. H. Henry, "Winds of Promise," *Christianity Today*, June 5, 1970, pp. 829–830.

13. Michael Harper, *None Can Guess* (Plainfield, New Jersey: Logos International, 1971), p. 154.

14. Michael Harper, "On to Maturity," *Renewal* (London, England), December 1972/January 1973, pp. 34–35.

III. A Thorn in the Side: Evangelicalism and the Contemporary Church

1. Dean M. Kelley, *Why Conservative Churches Are Growing* (New York: Harper & Row, 1972), p. 51.

IV. Backgrounds to the New Discontent

1. Tom Skinner, "The U.S. Racial Crisis and World Evangelism," in John R. W. Stott, *et al.*, *Christ the Liberator* (Downers Grove, Illinois: InterVarsity Press, 1971), pp. 208–209.

2. Elton Trueblood, *The Future of the Christian* (New York: Harper & Row, 1971), pp. 72–73.

3. C. S. Lewis, *God in the Dock: Essays on Theology and Ethics*, Walter Hooper, ed. (Grand Rapids: Eerdmans, 1970), p. 12 (from the editor's preface).

4. Quoted in J. Martin Bailey and Douglas Gilbert, *The Steps of Bonhoeffer* (Philadelphia and Boston: Pilgrim Press, 1969), p. 49.

5. Quoted by Eberhard Bethge in Bailey and Gilbert, *Steps of Bonhoeffer*, p. 96.

6. H. Richard Niebuhr, *The Purpose of the Church and Its Ministry* (New York: Harper & Row, 1956), p. 107.

V. Revolution in Orthodoxy

1. Quoted in "Asian to Head IFES," *Christianity Today*, September 24, 1971, p. 1166.

2. Richard J. Mouw, "In Search of a Theology of Politics," *The Christian Century*, May 2, 1973, pp. 501–502.

3. Quoted in Vernon C. Grounds, *Revolution and the Christian Faith* (Philadelphia and New York: Lippincott, 1971), p. 214.

4. Robert N. Bellah, "Civil Religion in America," in *Beyond Belief* (New York: Harper & Row, 1970), pp. 168–89.

5. Ibid., p. 175.

6. Will Herberg, *Protestant–Catholic–Jew: An Essay in American Religious Sociology*, revised edition (Garden City, New York: Doubleday Anchor Books, 1960), pp. 263–264.

7. Bennett, "Billy Graham in Oakland," p. 195.

8. Leighton Ford, "Is Man Really Lost?" in *Christ the Liberator,* p. 244.

9. John W. Alexander, "Where Do We Go from Here?" in *Christ the Liberator,* p. 258.

10. Carl F. H. Henry, "In and Out of the Gay World," in *Is Gay Good?,* W. Dwight Oberholtzer, ed. (Philadelphia: Westminster Press, 1971), pp. 111–112.

11. William E. Pannell, "Race," in *Our Society in Turmoil,* Gary R. Collins, ed. (Carol Stream, Illinois: Creation House, 1970), p. 31.

12. Mark Hatfield, "Sen. Hatfield: On Many Fronts We Have Lost Respect for Human Life," *Los Angeles Times,* August 8, 1973, Part II, p. 7. With respect to the question of amnesty, *forgiveness* (even *forgetfulness*) is a central New Testament demand. Upholding national *honor* is not.

13. Mark Hatfield, "The Sin That Scarred Our National Soul," *The Christian Century,* February 21, 1973, p. 221.

14. Alan R. Gruber, "Poverty," in *Our Society in Turmoil,* p. 117.

15. Ibid., p. 118.

16. Lynn White, Jr., "The Historical Roots of Our Ecologic Crisis," *Science,* Vol. 155, March 10, 1967, pp. 1206–1207

17. John Warwick Montgomery, "Evangelical Social Responsibility in Theological Perspective," in *Our Society in Turmoil,* p. 20.

VI. Toward a More Effective Ecumenism

1. Quoted in Waldo Beach and H. Richard Niebuhr, eds., *Christian Ethics: Sources of the Living Tradition* (New York: Ronald Press, 1955), pp. 489–490.

2. Quoted in "High Voltage Religion," *Melodyland Messenger* (Anaheim, California), January 1973, p. 2.

3. C. S. Lewis, *Surprised by Joy: The Shape of My Early Life* (New York: Harcourt Brace Jovanovich, 1956), pp. 228–229.

Suggestions for Further Reading

Books

Anderson, J. N. D. *Christianity: The Witness of History.* Downers Grove, Illinois: InterVarsity Press, 1970.

———. *Morality, Law and Grace.* Downers Grove, Illinois: InterVarsity Press, 1972.

Bass, Clarence B. *Backgrounds to Dispensationalism.* Grand Rapids: Eerdmans, 1960.

Bennett, Dennis J. *Nine O'Clock in the Morning.* Plainfield, New Jersey: Logos International, 1970.

Bethge, Eberhard. *Dietrich Bonhoeffer.* New York: Harper & Row, 1970.

Bloesch, Donald G. *The Evangelical Renaissance.* Grand Rapids: Eerdmans, 1973.

Bonhoeffer, Dietrich. *The Cost of Discipleship,* 2nd edition. New York: Macmillan Paperbacks, 1963.

———. *Life Together.* New York: Harper & Row, 1954.

Carnell, E.J. *The Case for Biblical Christianity,* Ronald H. Nash, ed., Grand Rapids: Eerdmans, 1969.

Clouse, Robert G., Robert D. Linder, and Richard V. Pierard, eds. *The Cross & The Flag.* Carol Stream, Illinois: Creation House, 1972.

Coleman, Richard J. *Issues of Theological Warfare: Evangelicals and Liberals.* Grand Rapids: Eerdmans, 1972.

Collins, Gary R., ed. *Our Society in Turmoil.* Carol Stream, Illinois: Creation House, 1970.

Davidson, Alex. *The Returns of Love.* Downers Grove, Illinois: InterVarsity Press, 1970.

Du Plessis, David J. *The Spirit Bade Me Go,* revised edition. Plainfield, New Jersey: Logos International, 1970.

Ford, Leighton. *The Christian Persuader.* New York: Harper & Row, 1966.

———. *One Way to Change the World*. New York: Harper & Row, 1970.

Green, Michael. *Evangelism in the Early Church*. Grand Rapids: Eerdmans, 1970.

———. *Man Alive*. Downers Grove, Illinois: InterVarsity Press, 1968.

———. *Runaway World*. Downers Grove, Illinois: InterVarsity Press, 1968.

Griffiths, Brian, ed. *Is Revolution Change?* Downers Grove, Illinois: InterVarsity Press, 1972.

Grounds, Vernon C. *Revolution and the Christian Faith*. Philadelphia and New York: Lippincott, 1971.

Harper, Michael. *None Can Guess*. Plainfield, New Jersey: Logos International, 1971.

Hatfield, Mark O. *Conflict and Conscience*. Waco, Texas: Word Books, 1971.

Hollenweger, W. J. *The Pentecostals*. Minneapolis: Augsburg Publishing House, 1972.

Johnson, Douglas, ed. *A Brief History of the International Fellowship of Evangelical Students*. London: InterVarsity Press, 1964.

Jorstad, Erling. *That New-time Religion*. Minneapolis: Augsburg Publishing House, 1972.

——. *The Politics of Doomsday: Fundamentalists of the Right*. Nashville and New York: Abingdon, 1970.

Kelley, Dean M. *Why Conservative Churches Are Growing*. New York: Harper & Row, 1972.

Kuhlman, Kathryn. *God Can Do It Again*. Englewood Cliffs, New Jersey: Prentice-Hall, 1969.

———. *I Believe in Miracles*. New York: Pyramid Books, 1969.

Ladd, George E. *The New Testament and Criticism*. Grand Rapids: Eerdmans, 1967.

Larson, Bruce. *Ask Me to Dance*. Waco, Texas: Word Books, 1972.

Larson, Bruce, and Ralph Osborne. *The Emerging Church*. Waco, Texas: Word Books, 1970.

Lewis, C. S. *The Four Loves*. New York: Harcourt Brace Jovanovich, 1960.

———. *God in the Dock*, Walter Hooper, ed. Grand Rapids: Eerdmans, 1970.

———. *The Great Divorce*. New York: Macmillan Paperbacks, 1946.

———. *Letters to Malcom: Chiefly on Prayer*. New York: Harcourt Brace Jovanovich, 1964.

———. *Mere Christianity*. New York: Macmillan Paperbacks, 1960.

———. *The Screwtape Letters*. New York: Macmillan Paperbacks, 1961.

———. *Surprised by Joy: The Shape of My Early Life*. New York: Harcourt Brace Jovanovich, 1956.

Lum, Ada. *Jesus the Radical*. Downers Grove, Illinois: InterVarsity Press, 1970.

Moberg, David O. *The Great Reversal: Evangelism versus Social Concern.* Philadelphia and New York: Lippincott, 1972.

———. *Inasmuch: Christian Social Responsibility in the Twentieth Century.* Grand Rapids: Eerdmans, 1965.

Morris, James. *The Preachers.* New York: St. Martin's Press, 1973.

Myra, Harold, and Dean Merrill. *Rock, Bach & Superschlock.* Philadelphia and New York: A. J. Holman Company, 1972.

Oberholtzer, W. Dwight, ed. *Is Gay Good?* Philadelphia: Westminster Press, 1971.

O'Connor, Edward D. *The Pentecostal Movement in the Catholic Church.* Notre Dame, Indiana: Ave Maria Press, 1971.

Perry, Troy. *The Lord Is My Shepherd and He Knows I'm Gay.* Los Angeles: Nash Publishing Corporation, 1972.

Pierard, Richard V. *The Unequal Yoke: Evangelical Christianity and Political Conservatism.* Philadelphia and New York: Lippincott, 1970.

Prohl, Russell. *Woman in the Church.* Grand Rapids: Eerdmans, 1957.

Pulkingham, W. Graham. *Gathered for Power: Charisma, Communalism, Christian Witness.* New York: Morehouse-Barlow Company, 1972.

Ramm, Bernard L. *The Christian View of Science and Scripture.* Grand Rapids: Eerdmans, 1954.

———. *The Evangelical Heritage.* Waco, Texas: Word Books, 1973.

Ranaghan, Kevin and Dorothy, eds. *As the Spirit Leads Us.* Paramus, New Jersey: Deus Books, 1971.

Ranaghan, Kevin and Dorothy. *Catholic Pentecostals.* Paramus, New Jersey: Deus Books, 1969.

The *Right On* Staff. *The Street People.* Valley Forge, Pennsylvania: Judson Press, 1971.

Roberts, Oral. *The Call: An Autobiography.* Garden City, New York: Doubleday, 1972.

Salley, Columbus, and Ronald Behm. *Your God Is Too White.* Downers Grove, Illinois: InterVarsity Press, 1970.

Sayers, Dorothy L. *Are Women Human?* Downers Grove, Illinois: InterVarsity Press, 1971.

Sherrill, John L. *They Speak with Other Tongues.* New York: Pyramid Books, 1965.

Skinner, Tom. *Black and Free.* Grand Rapids: Zondervan, 1968.

———. *How Black Is the Gospel?* Philadelphia and New York: Lippincott, 1970.

———. *Words of Revolution.* Grand Rapids: Zondervan, 1970.

Smith, Robert W., ed. *Christ & The Modern Mind.* Downers Grove, Illinois: InterVarsity Press, 1972.

Stott, John R. W. *Christ the Controversialist.* Downers Grove, Illinois: Inter-
Varsity Press, 1970.

_____. *Our Guilty Silence.* Grand Rapids: Eerdmans, 1969.

_____. *What Christ Thinks of the Church.* Grand Rapids: Eerdmans, 1972.

Stott, John R. W., *et al. Christ the Liberator.* Downers Grove, Illinois: InterVarsity Press, 1971.

Streiker, Lowell D., and Gerald S. Strober. *Religion and the New Majority: Billy
Graham, Middle America, and the Politics of the 70s.* New York: Association Press, 1972.

Ten Boom, Corrie. *The Hiding Place.* Washington Depot, Connecticut:
Chosen Books, 1971.

Two Brothers from Berkeley. *Letters to Street Christians.* Grand Rapids: Zondervan, 1971.

Williams, J. Rodman. *The Era of the Spirit.* Plainfield, New Jersey: Logos
International, 1971.

Wirt, Sherwood Eliot. *The Social Conscience of the Evangelical.* New York:
Harper & Row, 1968.

Periodicals

HIS magazine. Downers Grove, Illinois 60515: InterVarsity Christian Fellowship, 5206 Main Street.

Journal of the American Scientific Affiliation. Mankato, Minnesota 56001:
American Scientific Affiliation, 324½ South Second Street.

The Other Side. Philadelphia, Pennsylvania 19144: c/o John Alexander, 325
West Logan.

The Post-American. Deerfield, Illinois 60015: The People's Christian Coalition,
P.O. Box 132.

Renewal. East Molesey, Surrey, England: Fountain Trust, 23 Spencer Road.

Right On. Berkeley, California 94704: Christian World Liberation Front, P.O.
Box 4307.

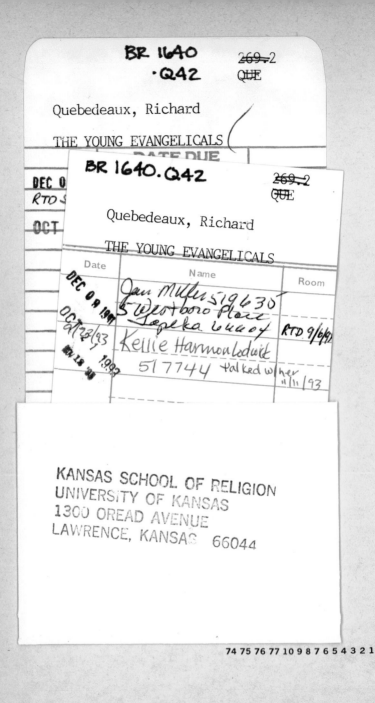